Simone

Titles in the series Critical Lives present the work of leading cultural figures of the modern period. Each book explores the life of the artist, writer, philosopher or architect in question and relates it to their major works.

Simone Weil

Palle Yourgrau

REAKTION BOOKS

For Mary

Published by Reaktion Books Ltd
33 Great Sutton Street
London EC1V ODX, UK
www.reaktionbooks.co.uk

First published 2011

Printed and bound in Great Britain
by Bell & Bain, Glasgow

British Library Cataloguing in Publication Data
Yourgrau, Palle
 Simone Weil. – (Critical lives)
 1. Weil, Simone, 1909–1943
 2. Women philosophers – France – Biography
 3. Philosophers – France – Biography
 I. Title II. Series
 194-DC2

ISBN 978 1 86189 798 5

Contents

Simone Weil in 1936, a volunteer in the Spanish Civil War.

Introduction

> To us a single act of injustice – cheating in business, exploitation of the
> poor – is slight; to the prophet, *a disaster*. To us, injustice is injurious to
> the welfare of the people; to the prophet, it is *a deathblow to existence*;
> to us, an episode; to them, *a catastrophe, a threat to the world*.
> Abraham Heschel, *The Prophets*

'More than once it happened: I denied Simone.' (*Il m'est arrivé plus
d'une fois de renier Simone.*) Thus does Sylvie Weil, Simone's niece,
born a year before her aunt's death, open her remarkable memoir,
Chez les Weil: André et Simone.[1] The echo of St Peter, who thrice
denied the one he loved, is obvious but unnoted, as is Simone's
own commentary on that famous denial: 'To say of Christ, "I will
never deny thee," was already to betray him.'[2] The power to stand
by what is truly good, what does not belong to this world, does
not come from within. To believe it does is a form of arrogance,
a betrayal in itself of what one claims to love. It is Simone herself,
thus, who has relieved her niece of St Peter's burden. Yet the
question remains: why was Sylvie Weil moved to deny her famous
aunt who had already, preemptively, absolved her?

Simone Weil, legendary French philosopher and mystic, died in
1943 in London at the age of 34, having forged in the brief span of
her life a Platonic reconstruction of Christianity – a bridge between
human suffering and divine perfection. 'The bridges of the Greeks',
wrote Weil, '. . . we . . . do not know how to use them. We thought

they were intended to have houses built on them . . . We no longer know that they are . . . made so that we may cross over them . . . so that we may proceed to God.'[3] Her *Intimations of Christianity among the Ancient Greeks*[4] Pope Paul VI would account one of the three great intellectual influences of his life; the others being Blaise Pascal and Georges Bernanos.[5] Albert Camus would pay a visit to her former apartment in Paris to meditate before going on to receive his Nobel Prize. Czesław Miłosz the Lithuanian-Polish poet, in his acceptance speech for the Nobel Prize, spoke of Simone Weil, 'to whose writings I am profoundly indebted'.[6] In a collection of essays,[7] he devoted one to 'The Importance of Simone Weil'. She has become, it is safe to say, a cult figure, a kind of modern saint, and yet at the same time a *bête noire*, a Jew accused of having abandoned her own people in their hour of greatest need. Having disowned her own, it was Simone's turn to be disowned by her own niece. Thus, a challenge: who is the real Simone Weil?

What is needed is not more history. Excellent biographies already exist, from the first and still classic by Jacques Cabaud,[8] to the very personal account by her friend and classmate Simone Pétrement,[9] a philosopher herself, to the recent, more psychologically focused chronicle by Francine du Plessix Gray,[10] to mention only a few. Naturally, the image of Weil that appears in each proceeds from a different perspective. Indeed, like the pieces in a puzzle, the disparate fragments of Weil's life can be reassembled to form any number of pictures or portraits.[11] The present study is not intended to add to this historical narrative. The pages of Simone Weil's life have been reshuffled enough in an attempt to reproduce faithfully her life's journey. What is needed now is an arrangement that convinces not by an attempt to approximate the original, but rather by a bold leap to get behind or beyond the surface, the veneer that blinds us by its familiarity.

We must attempt to imitate what Weil calls the 'artist of the very first order', who 'works after a transcendent model which he does not represent',[12] but which is only the 'source' of his inspiration. Weil's journey through life, then, for all its peaks and valleys, by this line of thought is not itself the 'real story' but rather a mere picture, a representation of something yet more real. Indeed, Weil herself sees not just life stories but the history of the universe itself in this light, so that what are called myths turn out to be the story behind the story: 'the foundation of mythology is that the universe [itself] is a metaphor of the divine truths'.[13] And Weil is not alone in this. As the philosopher of science Imre Lakatos has written: 'respectable historians sometimes say that the sort of rational reconstruction here attempted is a caricature of real history ... but one might equally well say that ... history ... [is] just a caricature of the rational reconstruction'.[14]

Nevertheless, a dramatic life Weil's certainly was – at once a tragedy and a comedy, as Flannery O'Connor has said – a journey without repose. Sleeping may be good for the body, but it is death for the soul. '[T]he soul is asleep', says Weil. 'If it wakes up for an instant, it then turns itself toward the legitimate form of union [with the divine].'[15] Yet for many religion provides a comforting shell to crawl into and slumber. Science too, Weil insists. She would agree with Wittgenstein: 'Man has to awaken to wonder ... Science is a way of sending him to sleep again.'[16] For these citizens of shells, these cave dwellers, Weil's reimagination of the Gospels in the light of Plato's philosophy comes as a wake-up call that tears away their protective cover, leaving them as naked as death. Indeed, 'truth is on the side of death',[17] writes Weil; 'truth is not revealed except in nakedness, and that nakedness is death'.[18] And it could well be said that Simone Weil was born to die. How often did she not recall her beloved Plato, whose Socrates claims in the *Phaedo*, to the alarm of all around him, that philosophy itself is but the cultivation of dying?

Weil's own life was bracketed by the two landmarks of death that George Steiner has aptly noted define the twentieth century:

Golgotha[19] and Auschwitz.[20] A child of both the Spanish Civil War and the Second World War, Weil's early preoccupation with the world-wide oppression of the working class – which found expression in what she once called her magnum opus, *On Oppression and Liberty*[21] – transformed itself into a feverish attempt to come to grips in mystical volumes like *Gravity and Grace*[22] with the sickness of soul that led to Fascism – more generally, with the degeneration of spirit that runs like a straight line from 'God and country' to the death camps of National Socialism.

A similar journey was undertaken by the Austrian philosopher Karl Popper – who, like Weil, devoted much of his youth to a critical study of Marxism – but with a different destination. It is Plato himself, Popper argued in his monumental *The Open Society and its Enemies*,[23] with the 'closed' society envisioned in his *Republic*, who is the ultimate source of the twentieth century's catastrophic neo-tribalism, whereas for Weil, Plato was not the problem but the solution. For her, Fascism as a disease of the soul was in the end not so much a political as a religious problem, and the root cause was idolatry in the form of worship of the collective, the state, which for her meant ancient Israel – 'the Chosen People' and their 'promised land', notions which Popper, too, considered 'tribal' prefigurations of modern 'closed societies' – and Rome, the ancestor of the modern super-state,[24] both of which, she believed, had helped turn Christianity, the 'religion of slaves', as Nietzsche also described it,[25] into the self-proclaimed ideology of conquerors. Christianity, thus transfigured, charted a course whose ending Weil coldly predicted long before it came to pass: 'In the thirteenth century . . . the Church set up a beginning of totalitarianism . . . [I]t is not without a certain responsibility for the events of the present day.'[26] Nor, for Weil, did the nationalistic cult of Joan of Arc escape responsibility.[27]

The proposal during the very years the Holocaust was taking place to rethink the heritage of ancient Israel has provoked, unsurprisingly, the wrath of many, inside and outside the Jewish faith, a fate that has also befallen Popper. Wittgenstein, too, has attracted the label of being a self-hating Jew, though in his case there was some basis for this.[28] The case for Popper being an anti-Semite is particularly absurd. In a popular book, *Wittgenstein's Poker*,[29] the charge is made against the Austrian philosopher on the basis of such statements as: 'I do not believe in race', and, 'all nationalism or racialism is evil, and Jewish nationalism is no exception'. It is a peculiar perversion to accuse an enemy of racialism and ultra-nationalism of being a racist on the basis of his not making an exception for his own race! Wittgenstein, by contrast, struggled with the concept of race, in particular his own, and found no easy escape via Popper's extreme rationalism (inspired by his hero, Bertrand Russell). Hyper-rationalism à la Russell, for Wittgenstein (as for Weil), was downright dangerous: 'Russell and the parsons', he said, 'between them, have done infinite harm, infinite harm.'[30]

Weil's rethinking of Christianity, in contrast, has engendered an extraordinary warmth of sentiment among 'true believers', for whom Simone, though never officially a Catholic, counts unofficially as a saint – though she could just as easily be compared with the ancient Hebrew prophets, for whom the smallest human injustice threatens the very foundation of the universe. The attempt to honour her with sainthood, however, would have been lost on Weil herself. 'I don't want you to do me the injustice', she wrote to a friend, 'of imagining that I affect saintliness.' 'I do not', she went on, 'like the way in which Christians today speak about saintliness . . . [I]t seems to me that saintliness is, if I dare say so, the minimum for a Christian. It is for a Christian what financial probity is for a merchant'. Of course, she added, 'there exist in fact dishonest merchants . . . and people who have chosen to love Christ but who are infinitely below the level of sanctity. Of course, I am one of them.'[31]

The suggestion that Weil be sanctified amounts in some quarters to a form of idolatry – i.e. the exact movement of the soul to which

Weil was most strongly opposed. 'My sister', said her brother, André, 'did not spend her life analyzing idolatry in order to end up becoming an idol.'[32] How disheartened Simone would have been to read Sylvie Weil's experiences as 'The Shinbone of a Saint',[33] where she recounts how her famous last name, coupled with her striking resemblance to her hallowed aunt, has caused endless ranks of the faithful to want to lay hands on her, to run their fingers through her hair. The family business? 'One cannot', notes Sylvie, dryly, 'take over the business of being a saint.'[34]

This hagiography of Simone has also provided a convenient excuse not to take her *ideas* seriously, a tendency of which she herself took note. 'Simone Weil's intelligence . . . [was] borne out by her writings' is how Emmanuel Levinas begins his essay on Weil.[35] What follows, however, can only be described as a dismissal, as one might swat an annoying fly – even if that fly turns out to be, in Levinas' words, 'a saint and a genius'. And in fact, as saint or genius, Weil, for all her cult status, continues to remain outside the groves of academe. As the centenary of her birth in 1909 came to pass, a striking movie about her life was in production, an experimental documentary entitled *An Interview with Simone Weil*, directed by Julia Haslett, in which Weil's powerful message of the importance of *attending to* or *bearing witness to* those who suffer is realized by interviews with survivors from Weil's past, as well as an emergent interview with the subject herself in the form of an actress (Soraya Broukhim) who gradually assumes the identity of the philosopher. An oratorio has already premiered – *La Passion de Simone*, completed in 2006 by the Finnish composer Kaija Saariaho. And a jazz CD by Darrell Katz bears her name – 'The Death of Simone Weil'.

And yet Weil remains a marginal figure. Paradigmatically, in the groundbreaking collection *Women Philosophers*,[36] there proved to be no room at the inn for Simone. 'I have . . . omitted', wrote the editor, Mary Warnock, a distinguished philosopher in her own right, 'the writings of women who, to put it crudely, seem to rely more on dogma, revelation or mystical experience than on argument.'[37] 'I have [thus] excluded', she writes, '. . . the works of Simone Weil.' Remarkably, she adds that 'I think that no one would dispute that the task of separating philosophy from religion is far more difficult in the case of women than of men.'

Yet one of the philosophers Warnock did not exclude, Iris Murdoch, reflected a different attitude to Weil. In both her seminal books, *The Sovereignty of Good*[38] and *The Fire and the Sun*,[39] the influence of Weil is obvious. Indeed, in the former she remarks explicitly at one point that 'my debt to Simone Weil will become evident'.[40] One can sympathize, however, with Warnock's position, since even though Murdoch herself was a novelist, she was also a noted academic philosopher, and her books assume a natural place in the contemporary philosophical landscape. Weil, by contrast, resists all categories. While it is not accurate to say, as Warnock has, that she does not engage in extended argument, it is true that argument was but one of her weapons – and 'weapon' is the appropriate term, since Weil is an extremely dangerous thinker. The same is true, however, of Nietzsche and Wittgenstein,[41] yet both of these thinkers (men, to be sure, a not incidental fact) occupy well-established niches in the philosophical canon. Indeed, one of the key tasks of a presentation of Weil's life and mind that pretends to any kind of seriousness is to try to provide a convincing account of exactly what kind of a thinker Weil was.

That is the task that will be attempted in the present study and, in pursuit of it, it will prove useful to find a figure to place alongside Weil to help us take her measure. A case will be made that the aforementioned Ludwig Wittgenstein – himself a mystic[42] and a Christian of sorts,[43] even, though it sounds odd to say so, a kind of Platonist[44] – is precisely one such character. M. O'C. Drury, a friend and disciple of Wittgenstein, wrote, 'after Wittgenstein's death, I became acquainted with the writings of Simone Weil. These have had as profound an influence on my subsequent thought as Wittgenstein had had on my earlier life.'[45] Other comparisons will follow.[46]

What will not be ventured in what follows is an attempt at comprehensiveness; impossible, given the scope of Weil's achievements. Simone Weil made important contributions to political theory, in particular to questions raised by Marx concerning social justice and organized labour, as well as to the problem of how to reconstruct France after the war. She wrote with great insight about the causes of war, and shone a bright light onto the reality of human suffering. She constructed powerful interpretations of Greek tragedy, especially Sophocles' *Antigone* – just how forceful has been shown recently by Marie Cabaud Meaney[47] – and also Greek epic, in particular Homer's *Iliad*, as well as Greek philosophy and theology. She introduced a new chapter in the study of Plato. She made brilliant but unsystematic observations about the nature of mathematics and physical science.

Quite possibly, however, her most original and controversial contributions are to philosophical theology, to the study of the relationship of God to man, of the interrelationship between biblical and Greek philosophical thought on the divine. She constructed a radical reinterpretation of Christianity along Platonistic lines, and in the process developed a controversial critique of parts of the Hebrew Bible. Yet if her mystical Christian Platonism can with justice be described as the focal point of her life and this study, it remains that her wide-ranging discussions are inextricably entwined, and one cannot avoid the tangle of the full web of her ideas. Our goal, however, is not so much to *describe* her thinking and the way she lived it as to *encounter* it – and her. 'A philosopher who does not take part in discussions', says Wittgenstein, 'is like a boxer who never goes into the ring.'[48]

1

Three Simones

My father had a double, a female double . . . My aunt was a double of my
father . . . I resembled my father's double . . . The day after my mother's
death, my father presented me [to some friends]: 'My sister, Simone.'

Sylvie Weil, *Chez Les Weil: André et Simone*

Simone Adolphine Weil was born in Paris on 3 February 1909, a
month too soon, in her parents' apartment, rue de Strasbourg, the
second child of Bernard and Selma Weil. Her brother André, close to
her in age,[1] would remain close to her in person and in spirit (when
far away) for the full length of her short life. Her parents were agnos-
tics – more precisely, secularists – who came from practising Jewish
households but harboured no sympathy for their religious heritage.[2]
Yearly invitations from her paternal grandmother to attend seders –
she kept kosher, and once declared that her granddaughter would be
better off dead than marrying a Gentile – went unheeded; hurt feelings never mended. Her father, Bernard (called Biri in the family),
was fond of telling mildly anti-Semitic stories. He was a doctor, an
internist, with a successful practice (mainly Jewish).[3] He had been
in the military and remained a firm patriot. 'No Jew prays harder
for his country than a French Jew', said Alexandre Adler.[4] The same
could have been said about the Germans. 'I am a German of Jewish
descent', Walter Rathenau said.[5] 'My religion, that Germanic faith
which is above all religions', he continued – before being shot to
death for being a Jew.

In all matters her father maintained a steady hand and a cool head, and never ceased advising both children how to attend to the health of their bodies, though their lives, it was plain to see, were devoted exclusively to mind or spirit. He was not bashful about recommending routines of exercise no matter what precarious situations his children had got into. It was Simone's mother, however, Selma (known as Mime), neé Reinherz, who ran the family. A highly emotional, deeply possessive and controlling woman, her grip on her children was tender but tight to the point of suffocation. Her own background was artistic. Her mother had a gift for the piano and Selma, too, played and was a talented and well-trained singer. Her wide knowledge of music was passed on to her children, both of whom came to adore the classical tradition. As they would become, she too, in her younger years, was a kind of radical (tame, by their standards). She once scandalized the other guests by pounding out *L'Internationale* on the piano in the lobby of a grand hotel where the four Weils were vacationing. Her childhood dream of becoming a doctor was quashed by her father. When her own children arrived, they became the focus of her life, and her ambitions. André, the elder, was able early to escape from her orbit – all the way to India, to teach – while Simone, the true revolutionary, could not emerge from the bosom of her family.

At six months, she took badly to her mother's milk – Selma was recovering from surgery – and became seriously ill. At eleven months, she took even more badly to being weaned, refusing food entirely, and nearly died. For all this, Simone always blamed her mother – in jest, or so one hopes – for having poisoned her through her milk, for having laid out for eternity a path of unhappiness. ('*C'est pourquoi je suis tellement ratée.*'[6]) A sickly child, Simone never really recovered her taste for food. Abstemious to a fault, she ate little and protested more, beginning early in life to use food – or more accurately, the rejection of food – as a political gesture. When she learned that soldiers at the front during the First World War were being denied their ration of sweets, young Simone abstained from chocolate. It was a pattern that would never end.

In the Weil household hand washing was not so much a recommendation as a religious ritual, and from her mother Simone developed a fear of germs that joined forces with an intolerance for the natural expressions of intimacy – the kiss, the embrace, the holding of hands. A mild eccentricity of her mother's – no kiss *ex familia* – with Simone, grew into an obsession. With the rare exception of a daughter's hug, for her entire life the embrace of the human kind, the milk of human kindness, was absent. A mere kiss on the hands of the young child could induce panic.[7] Sexual activity, needless to say, was never on the horizon. Even the specifics of her gender were negated. 'All these little girls' posturings and grimaces', wrote her mother to a friend, 'I'll always prefer good little boys . . . I do my best to encourage in Simone not the simpering graces of a little girl, but the forthrightness of a boy'.[8]

Years later, when Simone met Sylvie, she worried, just as Selma had, that the child might devolve into the dreaded coquette. Yet, as the grown up Sylvie notes wryly, Selma herself once wrote of young Simone that, 'I can no longer bear to see these young people flatter her, caress her . . . I am obliged to keep my eye on this little budding coquette'.[9] What in Selma, however, had been a simple prejudice was transformed by Simone into a life-shaping destiny. Raised like a boy,[10] she never looked back. Signing her letters, 'your respectful son', Simone became Simon – a favourite nickname for her in the family – a brother to her only brother, a second son. When, in the course of time, she wrote about the legendary Cathar civilization of Languedoc, she adopted the pen name of a man, the anagrammatical 'Emile Novalis'.

Inevitably this unsexing of self, this unhappiness with her body, gave rise to suspicions of anorexia.[11] Beyond dispute is that Simone was a stranger inside her own body – suspicious of the very fact of embodiment. And her body, in turn, betrayed her.

She was spectacularly clumsy. She was tormented by agonizing migraines that drove her to the brink of suicide, and by childhood illnesses and traumas the effects of which would never abate. She was betrayed by having been born a woman in a man's world.

Though she never ceased preaching the gospel of *amor fati*, she waged permanent war against the fate of embodiment. Constitutionally bad at physical tasks, she forced herself to engage in the most demanding labours. (Her work in factories would nearly kill her.) Unable to handle a gun, she insisted, as a one-time soldier, on being issued a rifle. (It would never have saved her.) Yet her greatest enemy, paradoxically, was her beauty. When still a child, she was traumatized when she overheard a visitor praising brother and sister: 'one is genius itself; the other, beauty'.[12] The observation hit the mark. She had fine, curly, black hair, porcelain skin and 'black, almond shaped eyes that suggested those of Byzantine frescoes'.[13] As for her brother, she herself would compare André's childhood to Pascal's,[14] a childhood that fully presaged his development into one of the leading mathematicians of the century, a colleague, in the end, of Kurt Gödel at Princeton's Institute for Advanced Study.[15]

Like her brother's genius, her beauty, too, was real, and visible – for nothing is more visible than beauty, whereas Simone's own genius was for years, less visible, yet no less real. As André himself confessed late in life apropos his sister's genius, he had been 'only a mathematician'.[16] There is no indication that the master of irony was being ironical. Yet ironies do multiply. While Simone herself in time insisted that it is beauty that renders visible the invisible realm of the soul, her own beauty she saw as only a burden, the one cross she wished not to bear. 'If thine eye offend thee', say the Gospels, 'pluck it out.' Simone plucked out not her own eyes, but the eye for beauty of her beholders.

Was this crazy, or was it deep? 'Simone's cross-dressing', says du Plessix Gray, reflected 'her need to disfigure herself into a caricature of the beautiful girl she could have been', an act of despair, 'caused by her general sense of unworthiness'.[17] Indeed, at school, 'those who saw through to her beauty wondered why she had chosen to make herself so ugly'.[18] She hid her body in men's clothes – more accurately, in clothes that de-emphasized her femininity – loose and shapeless. Like Joan of Arc, whose path, reluctantly, she would cross and re-cross, she was never forgiven for refusing to dress 'like a woman'. And like Joan, she would, once her body was safely in the ground – when clothes were no longer an issue – be sanctified, though not literally, as was the Maid of Orleans. Yet, as Weil quotes Plato,[19] 'all that is in the soul becomes apparent when it is naked, stripped of its body [never mind its clothes]'. Yet if clothes are so superficial, the mere surface that adorns the body that houses the soul, why do they matter?

They matter because 'there is no man', as she wrote later,[20] 'however wise or perceptive . . . who is not influenced by the physical aspect . . . *No one is unimpressed by dress.*' A soldier in her own war, her dress became her uniform, no less than the garments of her contemporary, the other Simone, de Beauvoir, whose path Weil would also cross, or double-cross, whose affectation of bourgeois 'over-dressing' – complete with lipstick and makeup – reflected her own plan, '*épater les bourgeois*' from within. It was a guise that Weil herself, whose courage and audacity knew no limits, was not unwilling to assume if the battle called for it, as when she interviewed in later life for a factory job at Renault, in an attempt to experience the life of labourers first hand: a scene that, if there were any justice in the world, would have been recorded.

Unasked by friends and chroniclers, however, is the question: why *should* Simone Weil have preserved her beauty? Was her disassembly of her natural good looks, her dispossession of her birthright, any different from that of the philosopher Ludwig

Simone aged 12, at Baden-Baden. The photo is one of three famous, and carefully staged, portraits.

Wittgenstein – born a generation before Weil but in many respects a spiritual companion – who went to extraordinary lengths to dispossess himself of his inheritance of his family's vast wealth, the unimaginable riches assembled by his father, the prince of Austrian steel magnates?[21] Money, a burden? Do not a great many people pray day and night for money and good looks? Not the philosopher, the mystic, the puritan. To the young Wittgenstein, his aspiration toward the philosophical life was blocked by a mountain of money that had fallen in his path. It is easier for a camel to pass through the eye of a needle, it is written, than for a rich man to enter the kingdom of heaven. It is no accident that Wittgenstein, a harsh critic of religion, would turn in wartime to the Gospels as a kind of necessity of his soul. Like Weil, he too would use his response to the threat of imminent death as a road sign to measure how far he had travelled in his spiritual journey.

And yet is not money something 'external', whereas it is the person herself who has beauty? 'A very beautiful woman', writes Weil in *Gravity and Grace*, 'who looks at her reflection in the mirror can very well believe that she is that. An ugly woman knows she is not.'[22] Weil's beauty was real, though it contained a lie. And yet there is truth, too, in Du Plessix Gray's reflections, rightly understood. For the philosopher is both subject and object, with an eye for beauty and a beautiful eye. That after all is the reason why love and sex have been, since Eve ate the apple, as much a problem as a solution. In the dialectic of desire, each of us is both apple and eater. Yet the beautiful, says Weil in a late essay,[23] is something 'we should like to feed upon, but it is merely something to look at . . . The great trouble in human life is that looking and eating are two different operations.' Indeed, 'it may be that vice, depravity and crime are nearly always . . . attempts to eat beauty, to eat what we should only look at. Eve began it.'

Eve began it. And yet are not the conditions for 'the Fall' the very basis of human existence? Even if, admonished by God, we were to cease to 'objectify' the object of desire, it will forever be true, 'on earth', that 'looking and eating are two different operations', and so we cannot but sin if we are to live. Insofar as Simone Weil was free of sin, then, she was preparing not for life, but death. We must come back to this, but not forget that the thorn on the rose was not invented by Weil.

For all her concerns about her striking appearance, her mis‑givings about her gender, her preoccupation with food, it was Weil's intelligence or, more accurately, her spirit that from the very beginning struck those around her. In hospital at the age of three, she 'astonished the doctors and nurses with her vocabulary and expression'.[24] More astonishing still was the three-year-old's rejection of the gift by a wealthy relative of a luxurious ring on the grounds that she 'disliked luxury'! And the child who spurned luxury would soon, with her brother, be memorizing long passages from Racine and Corneille. By the age of fourteen she had acquired a basketful of *Pensées* from Pascal, whom she would continue to love and with whom she would never cease to argue. She loved, too, to climb up onto a soapbox and recite from *Cyrano de Bergerac*. Her family could scarcely contain themselves on hearing young Simone declare, with full earnestness: 'Fairwell Roxanne, I go to die! I think it will be this evening, my beloved!'[25]

A romantic at heart, she was in equal part a stoic.[26] 'Kisses and embraces disgusted her', said Gustave Thibon, her friend, years later, 'and I never saw her cry.'[27] It was other people's pain that moved her, not her own. From early in life to late, no border could contain her empathy for the plight of others, from soldiers on the front lines to enemies subjected to harsh treaties, from workers in the luxury hotels in which her family vacationed to factory workers, slaves to machines, from present holocausts to those buried in the distant past. But what she could least bear was *separation* – holding herself apart from those outside, in pain. It would brand her forever. It would make her a slave. As she confessed later, it was only when she realized she herself was a slave and that Christianity is the religion of slaves that she became aware of her spiritual vocation. Unsurprising, then, that she would resist the religion of her ancestors, in which it is precisely the deliverance from the burden of slavery that is celebrated.

As a child, she would sit herself down in the cold snow and refuse to budge if her brother was given the heavier bags to carry.[28] Why should his burdens exceed hers? On vacation during her graduate studies, she shared the harvest in Normandy, heaving sheaves of thistles bigger than herself. 'Why the men', she would say, 'and not me?'[29] When the war came, she could never understand why only men should be asked to die. Hence her plan, never realized, of organizing a volunteer corps of front line nurses, aimed more at the sharing of death than at the saving of life. And hence her resistance, arrived at the gates of Catholicism, to enter, if it meant separation from those left on the other side.

She hesitated, moreover, to join a religion that might suggest that she wished to be separated from the Jewish people who were her heritage – even though it was a heritage she herself had rejected.[30] Exiled in New York during the war, she would similarly refuse to join her compatriots who from the safe shores of the Hudson hurled anathemas against their countrymen who had shaken hands with the devil in Vichy – the devil whom Weil herself had earlier condemned from the unsafety of occupied France. As her friend Thibon, with whom she stayed during the Occupation, wrote, 'I recognized the authority of the Vichy government, whereas Simone Weil was already a whole-hearted *résistante* . . . I have since learned that later on, in America, she defended the poor "Vichyists" against the final and unqualified anathema fulminated by certain emigrants.'[31]

Her horror of separation is especially striking given the distinction that would naturally be attendant on her intelligence. Yet is not intelligence, like beauty, a blessing? 'When my son was four years old', says Reb Saunders in Chaim Potok's *The Chosen*, 'I saw him reading a story from a book . . . He did not read the story, he swallowed it, as one swallows food or water ['I don't read, I eat', said Simone[32]]. There was no soul in my four-year-old Daniel, there was only his mind.' Horrified, he calls out to God: 'What have you done to me? A mind like this I need for a son? A *heart* I need for a son . . . *Compassion* I want from my son.'[33] 'Intelligence, that you can pick up in the street', said Wittgenstein to the critic F. R. Leavis.[34] Simone, similarly, would write in *Gravity and Grace* that when it comes to matters of the heart, 'the intelligence has nothing to discover, it has only to clear the ground. It is only good for servile tasks.'[35]

Though she disdained separation, it stalked her. 'Physically, she was a little child', said a schoolmate, 'unable to use her hands,

Simone with her brother, André, in the woods at Mayenne.

but of extraordinary intelligence . . . She felt like a very old soul.'[36]
The natural order of intelligence, the aristocracy of the mind
shared by Simone and André, led them in opposite directions.
He adopted a patrician's stance, the assumption of privilege, the
exact inverse of his sister. As a guest, he demanded of his host
the very best accommodation as a kind of natural right, while
his sister begged to be given the worst room that was humanly
possible, and chose always to sleep on the floor. And thus both
brother and sister, as Sylvie Weil notes,[37] succeeded in imposing
their extreme assumptions, albeit in contrary ways, on their
beleaguered hosts, who no doubt appreciated their departure as
much as their arrival. Yet Simone's friend Thibon is also correct
when he remarks that 'a Francis of Assisi or a Joan of Arc in res-
ponding to their distant vocation would never hesitate to make
their immediate neighbor suffer'.[38]

A lover of Grimm's fairy tales, Simone never considered them mere
childish fantasies. Her interpretations of them would later astonish.

For her, as for her brother's future colleague, the great logician Kurt Gödel,[39] the fairy tale represented the world seen aright. Indeed, for her the world itself was a book that, like any other, cried out for interpretation. Only later would she attempt to encounter the author more directly. Uncharacteristic of prodigies, her human sensibility, her compassion, melted into her intelligence. A separation between the two would be a lie. And a lie it would be to set Simone apart from André, her secret comrade in the rarefied world of the mind. Most observers could barely understand their private language, shot through with philosophical allusions and literary references in a variety of tongues, ancient and modern. (Fluent in Latin and Greek, they also spoke their parents' second languages, German and English. Soon, they would add Sanskrit. Other languages would follow.) When Simone the school teacher made headlines by her scandalous march alongside protesting workers, her brother, abroad, would address her in a congratulatory letter, 'Amazing Phenomenon', to which she would immediately reply, having a little fun at the expense of Kant (no easy task), 'Dear Noumenon'.

They loved and protected each other. André, the elder, would naturally defend his younger sister, but Simone, who never met a burden she did not wish to share, did her part as well. A fight broke out when she refused to let her older brother read a passage in Racine she considered too sexually explicit for his tender years. (An episode that could keep Freud busy for weeks.) In such cases, their parents would open the door to discover brother and sister locked in silent combat, faces white, each pulling the other's hair. At other times they would compete by reciting from memory long passages from the classics, a mistake earning its author, from the other, a sharp slap on the face.

André, however, had begun competing with himself earlier. It was he alone who had taken on the task of introducing his little sister to the world of reading. In secret, he subjected the five-year-old to study sessions, lengthy and demanding, and then, with suitable drama, astonished his parents when tiny Simone, out of the blue, began proudly to read from the evening paper. Other surprises, however, were less appreciated. The pair were no strangers to mischief. They honed to a fine point their skill at embarrassing their solicitous parents. Going without socks in winter and then declaiming their cruel parents' ill treatment to passers-by was a favourite prank that mortified their targets.

'*La Trollesse*', her brother called her, and within the family the label stuck. It was the first of many. 'The Martian', her teacher at the Lycée would label her, 'the Categorical Imperative in skirts', she would become in college, and 'the Red Virgin' she would be dubbed by her last professor before graduation, in retaliation for the humiliations she delighted in visiting on him. 'A combination anarchist and sky pilot' would be a somewhat friendly – and no doubt, accurate – tag she would also acquire. *La Trollesse*, however, she would remain to her family, and to the end their delight; although at the same time, unlike André – but in part because she was so like him – a problem. Gifted in mathematics, unlike André she was not a mathematical genius. Later in life, she attended the meetings of Bourbaki, the legendary foundational group of mathematicians her brother co-founded. One can only imagine the struggle she must have had to keep up with discussions she had no business attending – dialogues her brother would have glided through.[40] Gifted like him in schoolwork, unlike him it never came easily to her, and her test scores, while very high, were not, like his, the very highest in France.

Both children were raised as boys. Only André actually was one. As his daughter recalls, his tone when he spoke of Simone failed somehow to betray that it was a woman to whom he was referring.[41] Says Sylvie, herself, '*je ne la voyais comme une fille*' ('I didn't see her as a girl'). Success. And this woman who wanted all to think of her as a man, this Simone or Simon, remained in her brother's memory 'sacrosanct'. He would mime her to Sylvie and tell his daughter what he knew his sister would have said to her, thus making his daughter, through indirection, a partner to his fraternal discussions, an honorary second sister to her father or brother. Rejecting this sanctification, Sylvie would lash out about her crazy aunt. One wonders: if the dead Simone could so profoundly influence her niece's life, what effect would the living aunt have had? '*Ma mère disait souvent que c'était une chance pour moi que Simone soit morte. Je la croyais.*' ('My mother told me often that it was my good fortune that Simone had died. I believed her.') SW: Simone Weil or Sylvie, Simone or Simon, Simon or André. Three Simones, three lives entwined by similitude, by the fate of a world war, by the embrace of an early death.

The Weils dote on their precocious daughter. She is yanked in and out of the finest schools by an over-solicitous mother. One teacher is 'too critical and ironic'; others are just the reverse, 'too complimentary'![42] Home tutors replace schools, which replace tutors. Not the calm voyage of her brother, yet always she excels. But her efforts take their toll. She labours at night and strains her health to breaking-point. Her migraines begin to consume her. In spite of her father the doctor's prescriptions on health and exercise, her mother's preoccupation with food, the child Simone charts a lifelong course of sleeplessness and malnutrition. A balanced diet: equal parts caffeine and nicotine; food for thought, not life. The heavy price she will have to pay will become all too apparent, but so too will the vastness of the territory her mind will conquer. A searcher from the beginning, she lacks a true compass. She is going to meet her first, and perhaps her last, real teacher. 'Little wanderer', writes William Blake,[43] 'hie thee home.' An exile in this world, born far from home, as we all are, she will spend the rest of her life trying to find her way back. In her mystical story, 'Prologue',[44] written in Marseilles during the Occupation, she will describe an encounter with a mysterious stranger who takes her to a garret where he reveals truths 'she didn't expect', then abandons her onto the street. She longs to return, but has forgotten the path back. She is Odysseus, but can't find her way. With a gesture to Ezra Pound,[45] her true Penelope, it might be said, will be not Flaubert but Plato.

2

Six Swans

Acting is never difficult; we always do too much . . . Making six shirts out
of anemones and being silent: that is our only way of acquiring power.
Simone Weil

Sometimes six precedes three. Before the three Simones, there were
six swans. Practically from birth, it was clear that Simone and André
were bound for the École Normale Supérieure, the elite academy
which has groomed for posterity the likes of Louis Pasteur, Émile
Durkheim, Jean-Paul Sartre, Henri Bergson, Claude Lévi-Strauss
and Raymond Aron. One prepares for entrance into this most exclusive of intellectual clubs by enrolling in a preparatory 'cramming
school', known colloquially as a '*khâgne*'. André, naturally, enrolled
early and finished quickly – in one year, instead of two – passing
his final exams with the highest scores in France. Simone followed.
But whereas André caused few ripples in his smooth wake, his sister,
as always, stood apart. A student for three years in the prestigious
Lycée Henri IV class taught by the legendary Alain (pen name for
Émile Chartier), she cut a figure that few could miss. The once
white swan was darkling. The child who had been called 'beauty
itself' was hiding. The transformation would continue. During the
Occupation, her friend Thibon described her sadly, but beautifully,
as 'this shipwreck of beauty'.[1]

A tangle of black hair hid a pale countenance overpowered by
a pair of face-eating, horn-rimmed glasses. 'She looked', said a

classmate, 'as if she belonged to another order of being.' (She did.) Her garments, always 'with a monastic, masculine cut', told the rest of the story: 'a cape, boyish flat-heeled shoes, a long full skirt, and a long, body-obscuring jacket in dark colors'.[2] ('The Weils didn't do light colors', notes Sylvie.[3]) Her unusually small hands were singularly weak and clumsy. A chain smoker, she rolled her own cigarettes – 'the Achilles heel of her asceticism', said a friend[4] – but made a mess of it, so that there was often more tobacco outside the paper, and on her lips, than inside. Her pockets, stuffed with tobacco and papers, for writing, as well as smoking – assuming there's a difference ('this smoke has been transformed into pages covered with writing', she once told a friend[5]) – would be stained by a bottle of Waterman ink that she had failed to close properly.

Unusual for the time, she went hatless, but later in life, perhaps to keep the smoke from escaping, there was an inevitable beret, always the same. 'In Marseilles, in New York, in London, Simone was always wearing a navy blue beret', says Sylvie. 'My grand-mother wore the same one. Where did they get them? . . . Perhaps they bought them in bulk.'[6] Inside the nest of this alien bird was hidden a body that was intolerably thin, the result of a diet based primarily on starvation. Unhidden, however, were her marvellous eyes, piercing, all-seeing and unforgiving. 'She had nothing of us', said her teacher, Alain, 'and sovereignly judged us all.' The judge-ment came in a flat monotone, slowly, the words measured out with a coffee spoon, 'as if she were speaking in a foreign accent', as Cabaud put it,[7] as if, her friends said, she were delivering a speech for the Salvation Army – an observation that Leon Trotsky would repeat when he met her a few years later. It was assumed she was a communist, and indeed, she once said she had been a Bolshevik from the age of ten,[8] but in fact she never joined the party – though André said he had seen the draft of a letter to join.

The teacher of this Bolshevik-*manqué*, Alain, saw immediately what set Simone apart, and proceeded to set her and her friend

ID photo of Weil.

Je m'engage à observer le Règlement intérieur des Auberges, dont j'ai pris connaissance.

Signature du Titulaire de la carte :

Extrait du Règlement intérieur des Auberges

ART. 5. — **"Le Père** (ou *la Mère*) **Aubergiste" peut rappeler les jeunes voyageurs au respect du présent règlement et, en cas d'inobservance grave, expulser les contrevenants, puis envoyer leur carte individuelle au *"Centre Laïque"* aux fins de retrait.**

Simone Pétrement apart physically by placing them in the front row, at the centre. He was a stalwart Norman who walked with a limp, a veteran of the Great War, a constitutional iconoclast and philosophical sceptic of the first order. Descartes, unsurprisingly, was a favourite of his; his affection for Plato was less predictable.

Unintimidated by modern science, he showed little respect for Freud or Einstein, a trait shared by Simone, who extended this scepticism to Louis de Broglie (to her brother's chagrin), one of the founding fathers of quantum mechanics. Indeed, even her brother, when he had become one of the greatest – and most intimidating – mathematicians of the age, could not intimidate her, even, or especially, in mathematics.

For the Hebrew Bible, known to Christians as the Old Testament, with its fearful God 'who is always massacring', Alain had little use, but he found so much beauty in the New that, unbeliever though he was, he turned students into converts. He had a special affinity for the poor, the downtrodden, and himself disdained comforts, including the comforts of marriage, which he put off until late in life. He left his mark on all his students, and Simone was no exception. A mark, however, it should be noted, is not a mould. There is no secret source, no fateful influence that can 'account' for a person's greatness.[9] As Weil herself remarked apropos a chronicler of Marx: '[such biographers] don't present the life of a great man but rather the life of a very little man who by some miracle did great things.'[10]

Alain would assign his students a '*topos*' every three weeks, a brief essay on a topic of their choice. Good writing, for him, meant good thinking. Even more literally, good handwriting showed control of oneself and one's passions. Simone took the hint and forced herself to transform her customary scrawl into a neat if somewhat childish script which she maintained even to her final hours. And it was here, in her handwritten *topoi*, that this 'Martian', as Alain had dubbed Simone, returned the favour and put her mark on him. It was not a question of her brother's ease of mathematical discovery, the sheer scope of comprehension of this truly universal mathematician. It was a case, rather, of six swans.

Jacob Grimm's fairy tale places before us the story of a sister's love – the kind of love that preoccupied Simone. Later in life she would construct another remarkable interpretation of a sister's love in her commentary on Sophocles' tale of *Antigone*. Indeed, as Nancy Huston has noted in her 'Letter to Simone Weil',[11] 'brotherly love had always seemed to [her] as the highest pinnacle to be reached . . . Antigone, Electra . . . the girl of the "Six Swans". . . The women whom [she] glorified were young virgins with masculine qualities . . . never lovers or wives'. In the fairy tale, which every school child learns, an evil stepmother transforms a sister's six brothers into swans. The price for their return is six shirts sewn from white anemones. Six shirts sewn in silence, while the witch raves. Saved from death by the swans in flight, the sister clothes the white birds who themselves are saved, transformed back into their human likeness. An elusive story; a flight of fantasy. Yet, for Simone, in the handwriting of such myths could be found the hidden meaning of the world. 'Acting', she wrote in her first *topos* for Alain, 'is never difficult; we always do too much . . . Making six shirts of anemones and being silent: that is our only way of acquiring power . . . [I]t is almost impossible to sew anemones together and turn them into a shirt . . . [and] this prevents an additional action that would alter the purity of that six year silence. In this world, purity is the only force . . . Refraining from action: here lies our only force . . . and virtue.'[12] It is November 1925. She is sixteen years old. What theorem could she have proved that would have surpassed this?

Weil at the Lycée Henri IV, Paris, 1926.

It is sometimes said that Weil's turn, later in life, toward Christian mysticism was a dramatic shift from a life of radical politics, an unpredictable movement of the soul.[13] Nothing could be further from the truth. True, at the Lycée she was already active, politically, in the trade union movement, Radical Syndicalism, was even giving courses of instruction to union railway men (an activity she carried on for years). True, she shared Alain's scepticism towards organized religion, which he saw as just another organization based on power. No matter. The author of that *topos* is no less rooted in the sky than are the six swans. Later in life, she recommended Plato's *Timaeus* with its 'image of man as a plant [upside down] whose roots penetrate heaven'.[14] She already viewed fairy tales and myths as pointing to a reality beyond or outside history. She attended not to 'facts' (which make up this world[15]) but to 'meanings' (which lie beyond[16]). She would agree completely with Wittgenstein when he wrote that 'the good is outside the space of facts'.[17]

In the fairy tale Simone chose there is a force that rules the world, the world 'below'. It is not so much that it is a force for evil as that, *qua* force, it is ipso facto evil. There is only one way to counter it, by a love whose purity is not of this world, a purity that is strictly speaking, on earth, impossible – unless, through concentration, through the purity of attention, we rise above by wings of a special kind, wings 'of the second order', as she will write later, that rise by falling, that 'come down without weight'. 'Wings of the second order that come down without weight'[18]: in a single phrase, the very essence of Christianity, of the incarnation of the divine, of man ascending through God descending.

'We always do too much.' As she later writes, we cannot approach God.[19] We must wait for him to attend to us. We cannot ask him any questions. We must 'make six shirts of anemones and be silent'. If He speaks, we must listen. Acting is always easy; waiting ('attending') is difficult. All her 'actions', her political actions, will eventually come to naught. A failure? They point all along to inaction, but she cannot see this. When she confided later to a select few her mystical encounter, the truth is that it had already happened. She awoke at the end to what is most difficult of all: the fact that it is not 'help' that will attend us, but transfiguration. We must learn the hardest of all things to comprehend: to love, to die, not for what is strong but for what is weak.[20] Christ, she will write later, was killed 'because he was only God', because he could not 'help' us.

At sixteen, Simone is already Simone. The six swans are not alone in their flight. She writes a *topos* on Alexander the Great who leads a world-conquering army, but who also, when crossing the desert, refuses the water his troops have brought him, cupped in a helmet, by pouring it out on the ground. A simple story. A commander loyal to and sympathetic with his troops. Who would have made much of it? Simone did. 'Alexander's well-being,' she wrote, 'if he had drunk the water, would have separated him from his soldiers.' Here we find perhaps the most important concept in her life: separation. The great, one might think, are ipso facto 'above' and thus separate from us. For Weil, precisely the reverse is the case: what is good declines all separation. It is not because of his world-conquering armies that Alexander is great, but rather *in spite of* them. It is the universe inside, not the world around him, that is the true domain he has conquered. 'Everything takes place from within Alexander's soul . . . [I]t suffices to be just and pure to save the world . . . [as with] the Man-God who redeemed the sins of man by justice alone.' All the 'action', which is really inaction, is within. Only in this way, the way of the 'Man-God', that is, of Christ – called by himself, 'the Way' – is it possible 'to save the world', 'to redeem suffering men through voluntary suffering'. And then the startling conclusion: 'Every saint has poured out the water; every saint has rejected all well-being that would separate him from the suffering of men.'

Weil's Bibliothèque Nationale de France library card.

Not the world but its meaning is Simone's text. To the crowd, a great general whose soldiers bestride the world; as with the wild swans of William Butler Yeats, 'passion or conquest, wander where they will, attend upon them still'.[21] Whose heart would not be stirred by the sight of them, who would not be moved, like Gerard Manley Hopkins, to say that 'my heart in hiding stirred for a bird, the achieve of, the mastery of the thing'.[22] It is hard to resist the plume, this common test of greatness, so closely allied with political power and military might – except that, as Weil notes, 'our conception of greatness is the very one which has inspired Hitler's whole life'.[23] To Simone's eyes, however, there exists something different, more beautiful, more dangerous: a saint in secret, the true heart in hiding. Seen aright, 'every saint' in flight rises by falling. Then, and only then, as the poet concludes, do 'air, pride, plume here Buckle . . . , and the fire that breaks . . . then, a billion times told lovelier, more dangerous'.[24] Alexander, 'like every saint', pours out the water that would 'separate him from the suffering of men'. He becomes 'a billion times told lovelier, more dangerous [a threat to what rules the world]' than when he flies over the earth at the head of a conquering army.

The *topos* leaves its mark on Alain. But he alone is not the Lycée, and not all of Weil's teachers are impressed. She ignores history, which Alain derides, and her examiner is not amused: 'an intelligent young girl who evidently feels she is *above* history'. History retaliates. A low grade in the subject bars her entrance to Normale. She will need another year at '*khâgne*'. Where her brother took one year she will now require three. The battle is on. She retreats to the country to study, to repair the damage. In the spring of 1928, she is accepted at Normale, ranked number one. Number two is another Simone bound for greatness, Simone de Beauvoir.

Though she will do advanced work in Normale, it is in '*khâgne*', with Alain, that Weil's mind is forged. The anvil is Plato. It is there, too, that she struggles to overcome her awkwardness, the unnatural clumsiness of her tiny hands that never ceases to plague her. She joins the first women's rugby team in the 'Femina' athletic club. (Let it not be said that God lacks a sense of humour.) She is undaunted by the mud and bruises; it is her failure on the team that causes despondence. She will always be a threat to the team. When she later joins a factory as a piece worker, her awkward slowness will cause her fearful cuts and burnings, but they will cost her co-workers money. When she goes to Spain to take up arms against Franco, her command of the rifle she insists on being issued makes her a greater threat to her comrades than to the enemy across the line. When picking grapes, however, in her turn at farm labour, though spurning gloves to torment her fragile hands, she manages by sheer force of will to avert the threat. The harvest, to the amazement of all, is not slowed down by Simone. In all this, however, she never relinquishes her belief in the mysticism of work. For Simone Weil, as for Vincent van Gogh, the hand of the worker is the hand of God. Van Gogh's reworking of Millet's 'The Sower' could have been sewn on Weil's banner. And as with van Gogh, there will be an incident – in her case, unexplained – in which she holds a burning cigarette to her hand.[25] Van Gogh, too, will turn to God, serving as missionary to a poor coal-mining region in Belgium, where he chooses to sleep, as Weil would have, on bare straw in a small hut, with a special compassion – shared by Weil – for prostitutes. Unlike Vincent, however, Simone will not move in with one, but she will, dressed as a man, in overalls, accompany a friend to a brothel – which nearly costs her and her friend their lives.[26]

God is in the details, it is said. For Weil, as for van Gogh,[27] he is in the vineyard – close to mother earth. Indeed, especially in his early paintings, it is difficult to distinguish van Gogh's peasants from the earth they are working. In his famous *De Aardappeleters* ('The Potato Eaters'), there is a kind of alchemy in which there is as much potato (*aardappel*, 'apple of the earth') in the peasant as there is on the table. In Weil's alchemy, too, the transformation comes from labour. Her 'labour theory of value', like van Gogh's, owes more to St Augustine than to Karl Marx. Yet, with Marx, she comes to believe that it is precisely one of the sins of capitalism, of industrial society, that it not only separates the worker from his product, but more importantly robs his activity of its intrinsic worth and dignity, for it is 'work . . . [which] creates respect for the human person, and equality'.[28] For both, the opposition of mental to physical work is one of the great lies of the modern world. 'From the bottom of her heart', writes Jacques Cabaud, 'Simone Weil desired to work for the abolition of the degrading division between intellectual work and manual labor.'[29] And not just a degrading division, but the illusion of a chasm in epistemology. '[Even] to see space', she writes at Normale (to the amusement of all), 'is to grasp work's raw material . . . Geometry, like all thought, perhaps, is the daughter of labor's fortitude.' In work not only is the person himself realized but for Weil, it is there that his mind takes command. A Cartesian, for Weil it is not a question of *cogito ergo sum* but rather, *'je veux, donc je suis'* ('I will, therefore I am');[30] I bend my will to work.

Though her body is weak, her will, her desire to share the world's labour, is indomitable. While still in Normale, on vacation on the coast of Normandy in 1931, she longs for solidarity with the fishermen. To a man, they reject her. But when Marcel Lecarpentier 'saw [Simone] running along the shore like a madwoman . . . going into the sea with her wide skirts . . . I turned [my boat] around . . . and picked her up.'[31] She serves on board like one of the men – and more so. During one particularly bad storm she scares the daylights out of her captain: 'I asked her to tie herself down; she refused. "I'm ready to die," she said, "I've always done my duty."' A fisherman, like her great predecessor, she becomes a fisher of men,[32] and is soon teaching Lecarpentier's children their catechism and helping their father in educating himself in arithmetic and literature. For months after her return to Normale, he sends her his notebooks for correction. In this, she never stops. In her last few months on earth, withering away into a shadow in London while managing to write down thoughts that will amount to 800 printed pages, she never fails to correct the homework of her landlady's children, the younger of whom will fall asleep waiting for her outside her door.

Still at Normale, she helps found a school for the education of railroad workers and teaches there with her newly acquired friend, Camille Marcoux. Typically, she is oblivious to rumours that her relationship with him is more than friendship. Equally typical is her unreconcilable anger when she learns that in a class presentation, he relied on a text by Celestin Bouglé, a teacher she despises. To her, she tells her other friends, Marcoux is now dead. Invited to her home to play piano with her mother, Marcoux finds that Simone will not so much as look at him.[33] But she has other friends.

Revisiting Alain's lectures, he seats her next to his latest find, Maurice Schumann, destined to become a prominent Gaullist in the not too distant future and a faithful comrade to Simone (he will come to her aid toward the war's end). In time, they will become close, but as with all her friendships, this one too is 'platonic'.

Simone is ready for her life's work, but before she can put her ideas to the test, she needs to graduate. At Normale she is joined by three other women who entered the year before, including her friend, Simone Pétrement. Beauvoir, the third Simone, is at the Sorbonne, not Normale, working toward a doctorate in literature. Their orbits intersect but once. Weil's reputation intrigues Beauvoir, the tears she shed for a famine in China – and her strange outfits. Beauvoir's sartorial proclivities are no less extreme, though in the opposite direction: 'All my life I have been dressed in cotton or woolen frocks', she wrote, 'so now I reacted by choosing silk-style materials instead . . . and I always wore the same get-up, no matter the circumstances . . . Every morning I would [apply] makeup with more dash than skill, smothering my face in powder . . . applying lipstick liberally.'[34]

They finally meet in the courtyard of the Sorbonne. Only the revolution matters, declares Weil – her pockets stuffed with copies of the radical *Libre Propos* and *L'Humanité* – the revolution that will feed the poor. To which the reply comes, no less spirited, that the meaning of life matters no less. As their lives progressed, John Hellman has noted, each could have borrowed the words of the other.[35] In the moment, however, Weil looks her classmate up and down and intones, 'It's clear you've never gone hungry.' *Cyrano* again; end refrain, thrust home! 'I realized', wrote Beauvoir, 'that she had classified me as a high-minded little *bourgeoise*, and I was angry.'[36]

Only later would it emerge how much this incident, and Weil herself, would weigh upon Beauvoir, as well as on her life's companion, Jean-Paul Sartre (an earlier *Normalien*). Beauvoir kept in touch with Weil indirectly, via a mutual friend, the communist and aspiring novelist Colette Audry, who recorded Weil's extraordinary devotion to the cause of the working class – she would, for example, leave her salary packet on the hallway table for use by needy workers – while continuing to serve full time as a philosophy professor at a school for young women. 'Her intelligence,' notes Beauvoir, 'her asceticism, her total commitment and her sheer courage, all these filled me with admiration, [though] I could not absorb her into my universe, and this seemed to constitute a vague threat to me.'[37]

Neither Beauvoir, it seems, nor Sartre, could, for all their admiration, incorporate Weil into their life's view, a discordance unsurprising, as Hellman wisely remarks, 'in a couple who remained pure intellectuals, seeking a "meaning" for human existence sooner than addressing its sufferings and misfortunes'.[38] Indeed, as Hellman notes further, 'Beauvoir's basic search was always for independence, liberty and meaning . . . in a word, self-fulfillment.' For Weil, by contrast, the ideal was self-effacement or selflessness. Whereas Weil aspired to become a 'slave', Beauvoir's goal was to become a master, of herself if not of others. Where Beauvoir is the mother of feminism, Weil would reject even the label. Asked to lead a discussion group, she lashed out, 'I'm not a feminist!'

As an elite student of Normale, Weil was not required to take courses at the Sorbonne, and like many of her associates added disdain to absence. A particular object of her contempt was the Director of Studies, the sociologist Celestin Bouglé, whom we encountered above. Not content with embarrassing him in lectures (especially when the subject was patriotism), she cornered him for a contribution for the unemployed, and he acquiesced on the condition of confidentiality. Simone, who though passionate was anything but grim, amused herself by attaching a note to the bulletin board: 'Follow the example of your Director of Studies and become an anonymous donor to the unemployment benefit fund.' She would henceforth be called by Bouglé, 'The Red Virgin'.

She was equally offensive to the great scholar of Pascal Léon Brunschvicg, whom she chose to advise her thesis, 'Science and Perception in Descartes'. In her four years at Normale, not once did she consult him, a slight he was not likely to forget. Though surrounded by the greatest scholars in France, her principal instructor – apart from Alain – was herself. Her powers of concentration became legendary. She assigned herself impossibly long lists of study and disappeared for days at a time without food or sleep to devour her chosen texts. She carpeted her floor with books, crawling on her hands and knees from one end of the room to the other guided by her myopic eyes, her nose buried deep in the volumes, without respite.

Her writing was epigrammatic, suggesting Pascal – pregnant with meaning, but elusive. Her thesis was passed by Brunschvicg, but barely, an insult that did not fail to wound. Her orals, by contrast, on 'the beautiful in nature and art' – one of the central themes of her life – were attended by a crowd of students and received almost perfect marks. She would, after all, receive her diploma, her *agrégation*, and graduate Normale – none too soon, for all concerned. Yet Bouglé was not done. 'As for the Red Virgin', he said, 'we'll leave her in peace to make bombs for the coming revolution.' She soon sent a little gift to him – not a bomb but a postcard. Posted by Bouglé, against her wishes, to teach in the quiet little country town of Le Puy, she sent him a postcard of the town's claim to fame: a huge bronze statue of 'the Red Virgin of Le Puy'.

3

Au Revoir, La Révolution

[If] the Revolution is exactly what religion was for Pascal – a means of escaping the nothingness of one's own existence – it is much simpler to gamble, or drink, or die.

Simone Weil

At Le Puy Simone is accompanied by her mother hen mother to meet Madame la Directrice, so anxious she resorts to extreme measures: she adorns herself with a hat and white gloves. The meeting is successful, and, after much searching, so is finding an apartment. But in spite of her best attempts to set up her daughter in comfortable domesticity, Selma is overmatched. In sympathy with the unemployed who cannot afford to heat their abodes (or so she believes), Simone refuses to heat hers. Forced to accept a maid, she pays her such high wages that the poor woman fears foul play. Selma sends food packages and slips extra money to her daughter's roommate, but her efforts fall short. Domesticity is not Simone's forte. 'Does one eat bacon raw or cooked?' she writes in a letter to her beleaguered mother. At last, Selma capitulates. 'She's unmarri-ageable!' she writes to André (himself destined for a warm marriage and family). Unmarriageable? Could she really have believed, even then, that for her daughter marriage was still an option?[1]

Simone's teaching is more successful. Unconcerned with pre-paring her students for the '*bachot*' (baccalaureate), the certificate that will enable them to proceed to higher studies, her goal is not to fill their minds but rather – as Plato says in the *Republic*, one of the few philosophical texts she chooses to teach – to turn their souls. As Cabaud puts it, beautifully, she was 'far more concerned with forming than with informing her pupils'.[2] And we have witnesses. Jeanne Duchamp, a student of hers in the 1930s, says in *An Interview with Simone Weil* that Simone began her philosophy class by forbidding the students to buy any philosophy books – an unusual opening move for a philosophy professor – saying, 'I'll give you anything you need.' She came armed with her own copies of Homer, Goethe, Plato, etc., and translated everything for the class, Greek, Latin, German, English . . . everything. When asked for something in particular she took from the class, her former student recalls what Simone had said: 'When you decide something, always do what will cost you the most.' (Shades of Wittgenstein: 'Whatever you achieve', he once wrote, 'cannot mean more to others than to you. Whatever it has cost you, that's what they will pay.'[3])

There is more to her lectures, however, than such epigrams. Over the next few years, Simone will transfer from Lycée to Lycée: from Le Puy she will go to Auxerre, near Paris, then Roanne, near Lyons, and after that, Bourges. Always in trouble with the authorities, she wears this as a badge of honour: 'I have always regarded dismissal', she says, 'as the normal culmination of my career.' Her effect on her pupils, however, is profound. An extra class she designs, quite advanced, on the history of science is well attended by students who are otherwise allergic to additional studies.

What were her lectures like? Fortunately for history, some were recorded by a former student at Roanne in 1933–4, Madame Anne Reynaud-Guérithault, and published as *Lectures on Philosophy*.[4] Their content is remarkably rich and original, an unexpected philosophical feast for the fortunate young women who found themselves in her care. Though directed at high school students, they could just as easily serve as a text for an advanced philosophy course at a university. 'It is only those actions and thoughts', one lecture reads, 'which have a necessity about them that are truly human . . . A thought without necessity is a prejudice. But one has to distinguish between those prejudices which we can do without and those we cannot do without.' It is not for nothing that she has studied Plato.

The *Interview with Simone Weil* continues. Duchamp recalls Weil's unconcern for clothing, her dishevelled appearance. Others will remember that her sweater would be put on backwards, to be readjusted with the assistance of her pupils, who soon developed a special fondness for her. Her hands – her clumsy hands – stand out in their memories. With her simple, threadbare attire in winter, her sandals *sans* socks, she seemed a saint, or a medieval hermit. To them, the Red Virgin became '*La Simone*' or 'Mother Weil'.

Not all the parents at Le Puy, however, shared this sentiment. Besides their daughters' lack of preparation for *bachot*, there is Weil's high-profile participation in the Anarcho-Syndicalist movement, a radical trade union association, anti-communist, that advocates direct participation of workers' units in the ruling of society. Weil is active and highly visible in strikes, protests and marches. And she continues her alternate vocation – or perhaps, her central one – of teaching the workers. She becomes friends with Urbain Thévenon (and his wife), who have started a night school for blue-collar workers in the industrial town of Saint-Étienne, a three-hour train ride from Le Puy. For the next year, Simone (known now as 'Comrade Weil') will rise at 4 am on Saturday and Sunday to take the train to Saint-Étienne to teach the workers Latin and French literature. The conservative press provides a snapshot (of France, as well as Simone): 'Mme Weill, red virgin of the Tribe of Levi, bearer of the Muscovite gospels, has indoctrinated the wretches.'[5]

The press notwithstanding, Simone will soon, unlike many of her contemporaries, abandon communism to its hijackers in

Moscow. It will become apparent to her that Trotsky – her one-time hero – not to say Marx himself, represents not so much the solution as the problem. In the summer of 1932 she finally gets to make a trip to Germany to observe first-hand what she takes to be the vanguard of the working-class movement, which faces, however, the rising tide of National Socialism. Since childhood she has had a special sympathy for this country, feeling more outrage over the harm done *by* her country (in the Treaty of Versailles) than *to* it (in the Great War). Situating herself, naturally, in the seething cauldron of Berlin (which scares her parents to death), she sets out to visit factories and meet with labour leaders, as well as to encounter all she can meet in the ordinary walk of life. She becomes acquainted with Leon Sedov, Trotsky's son, and a prickly friendship develops. To her friend Thévenon, she praises the cultural level of German workers. The French, by comparison, are asleep. But in both cases their leaders have sold them out (to Moscow), and in Germany, they themselves are being seduced by the radicals on both sides, Nazis as well as communists. The sane middle is becoming an orphan. If this is true of Germany, she realizes, the hope for deliverance, the Revolution, is now but a bad dream. Only nightmares will follow. She publishes articles that leave no doubt about her views on communism and the German situation, comparing Stalin to Hitler, and laying heavy blame on both Lenin and Trotsky, which makes her anathema to the Left. As for the Jewish question, she is silent – a silence for which, after her death, she will pay a heavy price.

Back home, she begins teaching at Auxerre. Her attendance at labour conventions intensifies, as does the danger from her participation in marches and strikes, including, later, at Saint-Étienne, the famous 'march of the miners' of 1933. At a convention for the United Federation of Teachers, the Soviet delegation, with others, comes after her physically, and she is only preserved when her

Weil with her students and Madame la Directrice at the Lycée des Jeunes Filles, Roanne, 1933–4.

friends construct a human barricade. She has a proclivity for attracting danger. Her writing claims yet more attention. In 'Are We Heading for the Proletarian Revolution?' she proclaims: 'We wish to uphold not the collectivity but the individual as the supreme value.'[6] But on the left no less than on the right it is the collectivity whose star is rising. Weil, however, has embraced a first principle, never to be abandoned.

And she knows what it means to be a first principle or axiom. In her later writings she will draw attention to the harmful effects of modern mathematics – taken by so many to be the very paradigm of good thinking. There is too much focus on mere technique, on proof or deduction *from* axioms, as opposed to the search *for the right ones*. And yet God is great: 'God's mercy preserves mathematics from being drowned in mere technique.'[7] In her beloved *Republic*, Plato, her model for the true mathematician, will ask a question which Aristotle liked to quote: are we on the road *from* or *to* first principles? The road to her first principle, however – that the individual is the supreme value – will lead her to the ocean, where she will find herself in dark waters when she comes to reflect on the role of 'the collective' in the religion of her forefathers.[8]

Inevitably the personal becomes political. She forms a close friendship with a Revolutionary Syndicalist, the Russian-born Boris Souvarine, a rabid anti-Muscovite who with his mistress, Colette Peignot, publishes the magazine *La Critique Sociale*. A very deep friendship. There is speculation that this is as close as she will come to romance. Inevitably she is caught in the psycho-sexual web of her friends' relationship. Peignot's sado-masochism leads her, in her own words, to 'create a hell in sexuality',[9] and Simone devotes endless hours to helping her friend's friend recover from her abuses, including scheduling visits with Dr Weil. Simone Weil is receiving another kind of education. Three will become four when Peignot leaps from the frying pan into the fire, switching from Souvarine to the infamous Georges Bataille, with whom Weil herself will cross swords. When Bataille, in a review of André Malraux's novel *Man's Fate*, bemoans the author's lack of enthusiasm for revolution, for which Bataille himself has a kind of fetish, Weil pens an unpublished reply, sewn together from a variety of threads from her life. 'For Malraux's heroes', she writes, 'the revolution is exactly what religion was for Pascal – a means of escaping the nothingness of one's own existence . . . If it is simply a matter of fleeing from oneself, it is much simpler to gamble, or drink, or die.'[10] Bataille, for his part, is fascinated, if not by her ideas then by her personality. He finds her simultaneously 'repellent' and a 'true beauty', 'always black – black clothes, raven's wing hair, pallid skin'. She is, he claims (correctly), Don Quixote, and possesses 'an extreme courage that attracts her to the impossible.'

The personal becomes political. During the Christmas break of 1933 Simone (following a familiar pattern) invites Leon Trotsky, driven out of Germany and forbidden by France from holding meetings at his own home, to take advantage of her parents' apartment – a spacious flat on rue Auguste Comte into which the family had moved in 1929, occupying the sixth and seventh floors, with a view of the Eiffel Tower and the rooftops of the Opéra and the Louvre. The master of revolution – who has already sparred with Simone in print – arrives *chez Weil* on Christmas Eve, accompanied by two armed bodyguards. One is a very young Jean van Heijenoort, who will transform himself in later life into a mathematical logician who will assemble the monumental collection of historical papers *From Frege to Gödel*,[11] to this day a mainstay in the field.[12]

Simone requests a private session, the door closes, and soon her parents can hear him screaming. Not Simone, however, whose implacable monotone no doubt helps inspire the yelling. 'This child', says Trotsky's wife, 'is holding her own with Trotsky!'[13] Some child. In notes she wrote down after the meeting, Simone reveals what happened. She had reproached the revolutionary for his reputed role in the brutal retaliation against the Kronstadt sailors who had mounted a revolt in 1921. To berate a man whose hands had been soaked in blood in a fight to the death against men whose hands were soaked in blood must have seemed to an exasperated Trotsky not just counter-revolutionary but downright *petit bourgeois*. 'Bloody acts of retribution', he had once said, 'are as inevitable as the recoil of a gun'. 'Why did you invite me?', he had yelled at her. 'Do you belong to the Salvation Army?' Not the first time, one recalls, that the accusation had been directed at Weil. And Trotsky would not be the last military leader to dismiss his detractors for confusing his army with the Salvation Army.[14] His own meeting, however, had gone well. 'You'll be able to say', he commented to Mme Weil, on departing, 'that it was in your house that the Fourth International was founded' – an honour that was no doubt lost on both mother and daughter.

While the activist Trotsky continued to theorize about the conditions of the working class, the intellectual Weil decided in the spring of 1934 to experience it first hand. She asked for a year's leave from her teaching duties so that she could become one with the unskilled who work in factories, the 'slaves' of industrial labour. Nor did the Red Virgin neglect theory. She would write that year, in six months, what she would later describe with mock grandi - osity as her 'magnum opus', a long essay, 'On Oppression and Liberty'. It is not economic force, she argues against Marx, which drives human history, but force as such – that is, power. Already in Homer's *Iliad*, she declares, the domination of human life by the blindness of force is revealed. (In time she will devote one of her most famous essays to this: 'The *Iliad*: Poem of Force'.)

We seek freedom from the oppressive forces of nature only to enslave ourselves to the very means we have created to free our- selves from our previous oppression. The bad news is that our very progress is self-defeating, for two closely related reasons. 'Power . . . is only a means, a means of action', and thus the search for power will always be incomplete, will always fail: 'power-seeking [reveals] . . . its essential incapacity to seize hold of its object . . . and finally comes . . . to take the place of all ends.'[15] Marx, correctly understood with the assistance of Aristotle, had made a similar diagnosis of the paradox of capitalism in which money, which in itself represents not an *actual* good – like housing, food, understanding or beauty – but the mere *potential* to acquire such goods, is transformed, magically, into the good itself. Potentiality replaces actuality. Means replace ends. Just as in science and mathematics, the search for proofs replaces the justification of axioms.[16]

The other contradiction implicit in man's search for power, which Weil calls its self-contained 'seed of death', is that 'the spur of competition forces it to go ever farther and farther, that is to say, to go beyond the limits within which it can be effectively exercised'.[17] The contradiction is 'made up of the opposition of the necessarily *limited* character of the material bases of power and the necessarily *unlimited* character of the race for power . . .'.[18] Once again one sees the influence of Plato, for whom the opposition between the limited and the unlimited lies at the very foundation of the universe. It follows that the revolt against power will lead only to greater enslavement to a still greater power.

To these principles, Weil asserts, the Russian Revolution is no exception. 'The institutions arising out of [this] insurrection', she writes, 'did not perhaps effectively function for as long as a single morning; . . . the real forces, namely big industry, the police, the army, the bureaucracy, far from being smashed by the Revolution, attained, thanks to it, a power unknown in other countries.'[19] And herein lies, perhaps, the greatest danger. The way out, a false way, is to put one's faith in what may be the greatest force of all, the one that will liberate us from all others – the force of the collective. Yet, warns Weil, 'the expressions "collective soul", "collective thought", so commonly employed nowadays [by National Socialists no less than Communists], are altogether devoid of meaning . . . Several human minds cannot become united in one collective mind.'[20] Hence, 'we must', she concludes her essay, 'reaffirm on our own account, beyond the control of *the social idol*, the original pact between *the individual mind* and the universe.'

The essay is completed in November 1934, destined for Souvarine and Peignot's journal, which, unfortunately, like their relationship, has ceased to exist. It will be published in the late 1940s by Albert Camus, who will write that 'western social and political thought has not produced anything more valuable since Marx'.[21] Meanwhile, Weil is determined to take the year's leave she has been granted and, unlike the captains of Bolshevism, to actually put herself to work in a factory: 'the great Bolshevik leaders proposed to create a free working class, [yet] none of them – certainly not Trotsky, and I don't think Lenin either – had ever set foot inside a factory.'[22] However, this is easier said than done. First you must be hired. Her friendship with Souvarine comes to the rescue. He convinces Auguste Detoeuf, the forward-looking director of the industrial firm Alsthom, to hire the maverick philosophy professor/labour activist to work in one of his Paris plants on rue Lecourbe, and on the first Tuesday of December 1934 Simone's long awaited journey begins. She will never be the same again. Her youth, she will write later, will be killed.

Simone was joining ranks with the most disenfranchised members of the labour force. 'As a female worker,' she wrote later, 'I was in a doubly inferior position, liable to have my dignity hurt not only by superiors but also, as a woman, by the workmen. (And please note that I had no idiotic susceptibility about the traditional kind of jokes in factories.)'[23] Although she would affirm that the greatest harm was to her dignity ('the dread, always, of a scolding; one would expose oneself to a good bit of suffering to avoid a scolding'[24]), her body too received no end of cuts and burns. 'Imagine me standing before a huge furnace', she wrote to a friend, 'that spits out huge flames and blasts of hot air which blow straight into my face . . . I must never let the pain of this burning air on my face and arms (I still bear its scars) lead me to a false motion . . . I withdraw red-hot bobbins, drawing them out very fast to make sure they don't melt altogether'.[25]

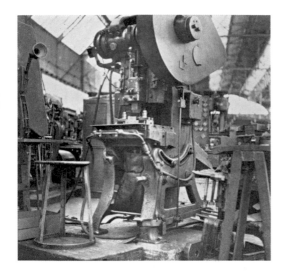

The type of machinery operated by Weil when she worked in factories, 1934–5, here at Alsthom's rue Lecourbe plant, Paris.

She was engaged in so-called 'piece work', whereby payment was not by the hour but rather the amount of work accomplished, which meant quotas that were strictly enforced by foremen who did not wish to see their totals decline. Speed was of the essence, danger irrelevant. Despite her clumsiness, she demonstrates some facility and is proud of her accomplishments. But the need for speed is unrelenting and the inevitable result is failure. Her loss of self-respect is catastrophic. What scares her most is not her inclination to anger but rather the more lethal sense of resignation. More and more she describes herself as a slave, and becomes painfully aware that the dream of a revolution arising from such slaves is a luxury she can no longer afford.

Sick leave, and then another factory, Carnaud, in the Boulogne-Billancourt district, making oilcans and gas masks. 'A penal institution', she calls it, 'a foul, very foul institution – frantic speedup, a profusion of cut fingers . . . I never once saw a worker lift her eyes off her work . . .'.[26] Once again, 'the object of dread was this business of orders . . . How one would love to be able to leave one's soul in the little box where one places one's clocking ticket, and take it up again upon leaving!' To make things worse, she is determined to live on her salary and take nothing from her parents, not money, food, nor housing. The result is unavoidable: 'I decided to spend no more than 3 fr. 50 a day in all, including transportation. Hunger becomes a permanent condition.' She is laid off and seeks a third position – this time without success. Finally, in line at a Renault plant, she overhears a rumour that the man who does the hiring favours the pretty applicants. Desperate times call for desperate measures. She persuades her friend, Simone Pétrement, to help her apply some makeup. Lipstick and rouge, Beauvoir's tools, become, for a short while, Weil's own weapons of choice. Pétrement is shocked: her friend is 'transformed into a beauty'.

The interview at Renault is a success. She will work from two-thirty in the afternoon until ten at night at the milling machine – a dangerous contraption on which she proceeds to cut herself badly. The headaches grow more violent, and she continues to count the pitiful francs she can spare for food ('eat a bun in the morning, another at noon, three more little ones at night'). She develops a powerful new concept that will dominate the rest of her life, *le malheur* or affliction. Whereas *la douleur* represents pain or oppression that can be a trauma, it is a trauma that one can survive: one grits one's teeth, screws one's courage to the sticking-place and ploughs through. The body recovers and the soul remains unmarked. *Le malheur*, by contrast, afflicts body and soul. One does not 'get over' it. It crushes the spirit, not least by humiliation. It brands one a slave for life.

Yet it is precisely *le malheur*, she will later write, that is a gift from God, for it is only in affliction, this 'marvel of divine technique', that one has a chance to make contact with God, as in the story of Job (one of her true heroes). As Pascal once said, there is in man an 'infinite abyss [that] can be filled only with an infinite

Photograph for Weil's identity card at the Renault plant, 1935.

. . . object'.[27] We cannot bear to be empty, our hands must be full, and yet, as St Augustine says, 'God wants to give us something, but cannot . . . because our hands are full – there's nowhere to put it.'[28] Making room for God, Weil is emptying her hands.

In August 1935 she is dismissed from Renault, but the damage – and the gift – is accomplished. She has followed her advice to her students: she has done what has cost her the most. Her idealistic illusions are being burned away. There are more to come. The limits of the political are becoming increasingly evident. And her frail body has only begun to be tortured. It is amazing how long it survived. 'There are some words in Isaiah', she writes to Maurice Schumann toward the end of her life, 'which are terrible to me: They that love God "shall run and not be weary; and they shall walk and not faint." This makes it physically impossible for me to forget, even for a moment, that I am not of their number.'[29] But she was. Until the very end, her body, in spite of being starved, cut, burned and even boiled in oil, never failed her. Each time it threatened to fall, something else held her up.

4

A Lesson in War

I loved my banner forty times more than my sword.
Joan of Arc

In August 1935, to help reassemble their daughter, fractured into pieces by her year in the factories, the Weils brought her to vacation on the coast of Portugal. She soon abandoned the beaten path and made out on her own for a little fishing town between Porto and Viana do Castelo. There, one night, in the moonlight, she observed the feast day of Our Lady of Sorrows, the women walking in procession on the shore by the fishing boats, carrying candles and singing melodies 'very ancient and of a heart-rending mournfulness'.[1] 'Christianity,' it finally came to her, 'in its essence, is the religion of slaves' – and she was one of them. It was perhaps her first awakening – to what she had always been.

Back in France, at her new teaching post at Bourges, her methods became still more unorthodox. She would provoke students by asking outrageous questions ('Have you ever killed anyone?') to startle them into thinking. They, in turn, with affection for Simone, who was now '*la Petite Weil*', would tease her by placing in her desk drawer some right-wing periodicals sure to set her teeth on edge. She asked them to read non-philosophers – Homer, Racine, Stendhal, Valéry – and determine their philosophies. Often, to the consternation of the townsfolk, who considered it beneath the dignity of someone of her station, she could be seen pushing a baby carriage for young parents from the lower classes. Her fondness for young couples was exceeded only by her love of children. She tried to get to know the working people, but her ceaseless questioning annoyed them. She asked to drive a plough, but succeeded only in exasperating the poor farmer by immediately overturning it. Her headaches, meanwhile, were driving her crazy. Suicide seemed the only option: 'every time I go through a period of headaches, I ask myself whether the moment to die has not come'. She did not fear death itself, but only wasting it. 'Death is the most precious thing', she wrote later, 'that has been given to man. That is why the supreme impiety is to make a bad use of it.'[2]

A better use of death was on the horizon. In July 1936, while she was in Paris, civil war broke out in Spain. She had visited that country and had a soft spot for it, and in spite of her pacifist leanings, which would evolve over time, she did not want to be 'in the rear' in the fight against Franco. 'I do not love war', she wrote later, 'but what has always seemed to me most horrible in war is the position of those in the rear . . . [F]or me, Paris was in the rear.'[3] Like a host of other intellectuals from Europe and America – including Ernest Hemingway, George Orwell, André Malraux and Georges Bernanos (who supported Franco) – she was determined to join the fight. She acquired journalistic credentials from a trade union magazine and set off for the front lines.

Arrived in Spain, she checked in with the Trotskyist POUM (Partido Obrero de Unificación Marxista), and then signed up for the militia of the trade union movement, CNT (Confederación Nacional del Trabajo). In Barcelona she tried to convince Julian Gokine, a member of the revolutionary government of Catalonia, to let her engage in an almost certainly suicidal mission to cross into the zone occupied by Franco to find and retrieve a trade union leader who had gone missing. After an hour of fierce argument, she lost the battle. It was not the last time she would make such an offer and be refused. In each case she was misunderstood. She wanted not to avoid but to find danger. A similar misunderstanding occurred when Weil's kindred spirit, Wittgenstein, enlisted for Austria in the First World War. '[There were] comical misunderstandings', wrote his sister Hermine Wittgenstein years later, 'which resulted from the fact that the military authorities . . . always assumed that he was trying to obtain an easier posting for himself, when in fact what he wanted was to be given a more dangerous one.'[4] As he himself wrote: 'If only I may be allowed to risk my life in some dangerous assignment. . . . If I'm standing eye to eye with death . . . I shall have the chance to be a decent human being'.[5]

The similarities, and the paradoxes, run deeper. Though he won medals for his courage in battle and was valuable in directing fire for the artillery, it is far from clear that Wittgenstein would have

In uniform,
Barcelona, 1936.

taken another's life in hand-to-hand combat. Years later, before D-Day, he had told his friend M. O'C. Drury that 'if it ever happens that you get mixed up in hand-to-hand fighting, you must just stand aside and let yourself be massacred'.[6] There can be no doubt that Weil, too, was willing and indeed did risk her life in the Spanish War – prisoners on both sides were massacred – and was willing to risk it still further, but there is considerable doubt whether she would have been able to shoot dead a fellow human being, no matter what uniform he was wearing. 'I continued on my way', says Lyutov in 'After the Battle', from Isaac Babel's *Red Cavalry*,[7] 'imploring fate to grant me the simplest of proficiencies – the ability to kill my fellow man.' Yet she was after all assisting soldiers who were doing just that – and a lot more. A student of paradox, she was well aware of this: 'If I'm captured', she wrote, 'I'll be executed, but that is what we all deserve . . . Morally, I am an accomplice.'[8] She was willing to die for her complicity, but not to kill. A paradox, but one for which even the greatest military heroine in the history of France, Joan of Arc, was famous. Though she led her army to bloody victories, when captured she claimed never to have killed the enemy with her own hands, proclaiming instead that 'I loved my banner forty times more than my sword.'

Sainte Simone, a kind of photographic negative of St Joan, joined a column of 6,000 men led by the redoubtable Buenaventura Durruti of the Catalan anarchist unions. She was accepted into a small commando unit of foreigners, the only woman. She asked for and was given a rifle. Carpentier, who had been a colonel in the French colonial army, taught her how to shoot, but during rifle practice the wise stayed well out of range. She begged and was permitted to join a raiding party that crossed the Ebro River, but thereafter was commanded to stay behind with the German cook. A deep hole was dug to hide a huge cooking pot at ground level, to keep from giving away their position. At night, the myopic Weil stepped right into the pot of boiling oil. A terrible burn rose half-way up her leg. The skin clung to her socks as her companions pulled at her boots. She was sent by boat to Pina, where her wound was attended to by a . . . barber. Somehow, she managed to get back on the road to Barcelona and picked up a ride. On her arrival in the city, she ran into her parents who were sitting outside a café. They had spent five anxious days waiting for her, with no news. Weeks later more news arrived. The volunteer unit to which she had belonged, which had grown considerably, had been smashed by the enemy. Every woman in the company had been killed.

Recuperating at her parents' hotel, she was visited by Carpentier, who related a story that burned into her soul. A fifteen-year-old boy had been captured, claiming he had been forced to fight for Franco. 'He was sent to Durruti,' as she told the story later,[9] 'who lectured him for an hour on the beauties of the anarchist ideal and gave him the choice between death and enrolling immediately in the ranks of his captors, against his comrades of yesterday.' He chose death, and they shot him. Thereafter he, who had belonged to the 'enemy', became for Weil her 'little hero'. His death – his murder – crystallized her sentiments about what the war in Spain really meant: 'One sets out as a volunteer, with the idea of sacrifice, and finds oneself in a war which resembles a war of mercenaries, only with much more cruelty and with less human respect for the enemy.'[10] It confirmed the impressions she had already formed. Two anarchists had tried to amuse her by recounting their tale of capturing two priests. Having killed one instantly, they allowed the other to leave, only to shoot him in the back at twenty paces. 'The one who told me the story', she wrote later, 'was very surprised not to see me laugh.'[11]

The person she repeated the story to was Georges Bernanos, a Franco sympathizer. In a remarkable letter written a year after her experiences in Spain, she told the great Catholic novelist what his book on the Spanish Civil War, *Les Grands Cimetières sous la lune*,[12] had meant to her. Her lesson in war had taught her that 'when once a certain class of people has been placed by the temporal and spiritual authorities outside the ranks of those whose life has value, then nothing comes more naturally to men than murder'.[13] It was a lesson that would apply all too soon to the coming war with Germany (the excesses of which surprised Weil less than others), and that already applied, for Weil, to the dark history of Christianity (from the Crusades to the Inquisition and beyond). But the light shines brightest in the darkness. 'I could not point to a single person, except you alone', she told Bernanos, 'who has been exposed to the atmosphere of the civil war and has resisted it. What do I care that you are a royalist . . . ? You are incomparably nearer to me than my comrades of the Aragon militias – and yet I loved them.'[14] Who, after all, is 'one's own'? Who is the real enemy? What set Bernanos apart from the others, including those who had fought alongside Weil, was precisely his unwillingness to separate his cause from his enemy's – his men, from theirs. Unblinded by his own banner, he never lost sight of the common humanity of men.

To be simply the enemy of one's enemy is not yet to rise above him. 'Good as the opposite of evil', writes Weil, 'is in a sense equivalent to it . . . That which is the direct opposite of evil never belongs to the order of higher good.'[15] . . . (Examples: theft and the bourgeois respect for property, adultery and the "respectable woman", the savings bank and waste)'.[16] Hence, 'the word "good" has not the same meaning when it is a term of the correlation, good-evil, as when it describes the very being of God.'[17] A Greek, in particular a Pythagorean idea: 'the good is always defined by the union of opposites. When we recommend the opposite of an evil we remain on the same level as that evil.'[18] Weil hints here at what will become a central theme in her philosophy: 'The correlation of contradict - ories is detachment. An attachment to a particular thing can only be destroyed by an attachment which is incompatible with it. That explains [what is written in the Gospels]: "Love your enemies" . . . "He who hateth not his father and mother".'[19]

That is why Bernanos stands out. He put Weil in mind of the lost wisdom of the Greeks, of Pythagoras, of Homer in the *Iliad*. 'The extraordinary equity which inspires the *Iliad*', she writes, 'where neither victors not vanquished are either admired, despised, or hated . . . has had no imitators.'[20] One is hardly made to feel that the poet is a Greek and not a Trojan.'[21] (Is there an account of the Second World War, one must ask, of which this is true?) 'Because it is blind,' she adds, 'destiny establishes [in Homer] a sort of justice, blind also, which punishes men of arms with death by the sword. The *Iliad* formulated the justice of retaliation long before the Gospels, and almost in the same terms: Ares is equitable, he kills those who kill.'[22]

'Long before the Gospels.' Weil discloses here what will be a principal theme of her later life, the fact that in ancient Greece (and elsewhere) there are 'intimations of Christianity', and not only in poetry. Yet more central is the (long lost) Greek idea of geometry. 'This retribution', she writes, '[is] of a geometric strictness, which punishes automatically the abuse of strength'[23] – as the conclusion of the Second World War will demonstrate dramatically to both Germany and Japan. In the present lost age, by contrast, 'we are only geometricians in regard to matter; the Greeks were first of all geometricians in the apprenticeship of virtue'.[24] God ever geometrizes, said the founders of modern science. For Weil this was true but misunderstood. What was meant was only that God is a geometrician of matter. The true God, for Weil, is a geometrician of virtue. The Gospels, she writes, demonstrate this; they are 'the last and most marvelous expression of Greek genius; the *Iliad* is the first expression'.[25] And then comes an idea at the very centre of Weil's interpretation of Christianity: 'Incarnation. God is weak because he is impartial. He sends sunshine and rain to good and evil alike. This indifference of the Father and the weakness of Christ correspond . . . God changes nothing whatsoever. Christ was killed out of anger because he was only God.'[26]

As she left Spain, however, lightning had not yet struck. She returned to Paris and to her politically activist ways, yet – those around her said – less abrasively than before. But in January 1937 Germany invaded Spanish Morocco and it was feared that French Morocco was next. War was in the air, and Simone could no longer stay quiet. She had taken her turn, as a French thinker must, as a café philosopher, meeting at the Café de Flore with a group organized by her friend Boris Souvarine and her former boss Auguste Detoeuf – a group that included Jacques Maritain and Denis de Rougement. In their new journal, *Nouveau Cahiers*, she published a bold essay, 'Let Us Not Start Another Trojan War'. (Her thinking, clearly, was forever marked by an Attic sensibility.) Just as the Greeks and Trojans, she argued, had fought over Helen, who in reality represented nothing more real than prestige ('what does Helen matter to Ulysses?'[27]), we must be careful not to relive that war over our newest illusion, that of French prestige. That she would one day run up against Charles de Gaulle was on the cards. 'Prestige', she went on, 'has no bounds [recall her earlier essay on limitlessness] and its satisfaction always involves the infringement of someone else's dignity.' Her solution? She had none. Her visit to Germany as the Nazis rose to power, her year in the factories as a 'slave' tied to a machine, her disconsolate adventure in the Spanish war, all contributed to her increased sense of an unavoidable destiny in human affairs. We are at an impasse, she declared, 'from which humanity can only escape by some miracle'.[28] Miracles, however, by their very nature are rare.

If her soul was once again up in arms, her body remained frail. Her leg had not yet fully healed, and her headaches cried out for treatment. She checked in at a clinic in Montana, Switzerland, to no avail, but she did strike up a friendship there with a young medical student, Jean Posternak, whom she attempted, assidu-ously, to educate in the classics. She was off, next, for a visit to Italy which she had long awaited, and her letters to Posternak would provide an invaluable record of her journey. If there was anything that took the place of food in Weil's life it was the beautiful. 'The aesthete's point of view', she wrote later, 'is sacri - legious . . . It consists in amusing oneself with beauty . . . Beauty, [however], is something to be eaten; it is food.'[29] And Italy served up a banquet like no other country. She gorged herself on Leonardo, got drunk at the opera. In her next visit to Italy, she would write that 'I'm soused, completely soused, from drinking in Giotto.'[30]

To Posternak she describes a hidden 'double composition' in *The Last Supper*, 'one in two-dimensional and one in three-dimensional space', and concludes by observing that 'there's no defensible reason not to spend one's whole life in that convent refectory'.[31] She likes Milan, and finds Florence 'my own city'. She takes time out in her own city to visit the headquarters of the Fascist Party, where an acquaintance of Posternak's informs her that her 'normal and legitimate place in society is at the bottom of a salt mine'. She attends performances of *Otello* and *Le Nozze de Figaro*, Bruno Walter conducting, and her favourite, Monteverdi's *Incoronazione di Poppaea*. She reads sonnets by Michelangelo and Machiavelli's *Istorie Fiorentine*, in which she finds 'passages finer than Tacitus, if that is possible'. She visits Bologna, Ravenna and Rome; attends Mass at St Peter's.

But it is the small town of Assisi that eclipses all others: 'at Assisi I forgot all about Milan, Florence, Rome, and the rest'. She is 'over-come by such graceful landscapes, so miraculously evangelical and Franciscan'.[32] Then, though she will not confide this to anyone for several years, alone in the tiny chapel of Santa Maria degli Angeli where St Francis prayed, 'something stronger than I was compelled me, for the first time in my life, to go down on my knees'.[33] She is having what she never suspected was possible, a direct encounter with the divine, with Christ himself, though it will take one more epiphany for the meaning of this experience to reveal itself. 'Every saint has poured out the water.' Properly seen, each moment in

An undated oval portrait of Weil.

her life has prepared her for this, not least the transcendent beauty she has just experienced in her Italian journey, for 'there is as it were an incarnation of God in the world', as she will write later, 'and it is indicated by beauty. The beautiful is the experimental proof of God.'[34]

Unaware as yet that her life has made a crucial turn, she returns to France and resumes teaching, this time in the industrial town of Saint-Quentin, within easy reach of Paris, as she had always wanted. The situation is good, but the news is bad. Franco has just captured the northern town of Bilbao. The Republican cause is lost. And her headaches have returned. To her mother's consternation, she visits a surgeon, suspecting a brain tumour. Still no relief. Finally, in January 1938, she is forced to request a leave from teaching, then again for the school year 1938–9 and yet again for 1939–40. Her lesson in war has ended. Her teaching career is over.

5

A Great Day for Indo-China

[A] prejudice is necessary for patriotism. He who finds it necessary to
conduct an unbiased examination of all people to make up his mind as
to who is best knows no true patriotism.

Gottlob Frege

You may expect an individual to display this sort of tolerance [for a
blemish on the body, or the body-politic, as Jews have been regarded] . . .
but you cannot expect this of a nation, since it is only a nation by virtue
of not disregarding such things.

Ludwig Wittgenstein

As all around Europe the ground was trembling from the rumble
of tanks, Weil attended increasingly to the tremors stirring inside
herself. She decided in the spring of 1938 to visit the Benedictine
abbey of Solesmes, known for its wonderful plain chant. Sitting in
the back row, she attended services 'religiously', putting others to
shame. Though 'each sound hurt me like a blow', she was able to
marshal her extraordinary powers of concentration to go beyond
the pain and focus on the simple beauty of the chanting, and on
'the possibility of divine love in the midst of affliction'.[1] She be-
friended a young Englishman, her 'angel boy',[2] and was introduced
to the English metaphysical poets. She became especially attached
to George Herbert's poem 'Love', and could not stop reading it.[3]
(Her English, it goes without saying, was excellent.) 'Love bade me

welcome', the poem begins, 'yet my soul drew back, Guiltie of dust and sin.' The unique style of this poetry was new to Simone, and more so its effect, with its mystical ending: 'You must sit down, sayes Love, and taste my meat. So I did sit and eat.' As always, it was not eating as activity but rather as idea or metaphor that moved her. It was the same with sexual union, an image she frequently invoked. Not, however, with love, since there, arguably, there is a convergence between concept and object. Whereas, as Weil's own life demonstrates, a chasm separates sex from the idea or possibility of sex, the idea of love is love itself. It's not that thinking you love your friend means that you do love her, but rather that if you really do grasp what it would be to fall in love, you are thereby 'in touch with' its reality. And the same, perhaps, is true of God.

That the very possibility of God implies His actuality is the basis of the so-called 'ontological argument', which Weil calls the 'argument from perfection', and to which she subscribes. Does not St John's Gospel open with the words: 'In the beginning was the Word, and the Word was with God, and the Word *was* God'? Between Christ (or God) and the idea (*logos*) of Christ there is no distinction. St John's Gospel, it should be recalled, is known as the philosophical one because of its Platonic resonances. This is no doubt part of the reason Weil loved it – whereas Wittgenstein liked it least of all, saying he was 'one hundred per cent Hebraic [vs. Greek]'. ('Hebraic' though he may have been, however, he also said that the Hebrew Bible meant nothing to him – whereas in the trenches in the First World War, he was never without a copy of the Gospels in his backpack.)

Returned to Paris, Weil felt while reciting the poem, which she now knew by heart, in the midst of a terrible headache, 'while completely unprepared for it (I had never read the mystics), a presence more personal, more certain, more real than that of a human being.' At first she had thought it was only the beauty of the words that was affecting her, but then 'Christ Himself came down and He took me.'[4] From then on, she averred, 'the name of God and the name of Christ' were 'irresistibly mingled'.[5] Yet, though it was specifically Christ's name that she invoked, what is striking is that she responded by seeking immediately to enlarge and universalize her experience, inaugurating a sustained search to find what is common to all religions – whereas for most people, a turn toward religion signifies an inclination toward exclusivity, a belief in the superiority of one's own form of worship and its dissonance with all others.

For Simone Weil, by contrast, exclusivity – that is, *separation* – represented the very antithesis of true religion. As for actual religious practice, she would have agreed with Woody Allen's character in his movie *Deconstructing Harry* (1997), who confronts his orthodox sister: 'They're clubs. They're exclusionary. They foster the concept of 'the other' . . . so you know who to hate.' With him, she would have asked, 'If a Jew gets massacred . . . does it bother you more than if it's a Gentile?' And if she too heard the reply, 'Yes, they're my people', she too would have responded that 'they're *all* your people.' And she too would in fact be confronted, before and also long after her death, with the final, damning response: 'You're a self-hating Jew.'

Weil's wide-ranging studies took her from the Egyptian *Book of the Dead* to sacred texts from the Assyro-Babylonian tradition, to the *Bhagavad Gita* – in which her brother had long since immersed himself – to a re-examination of the Old Testament.[6] For this, perversely, she has been taken to task, accused even by a sympathetic biographer of 'scavenging from multiple sources' (as if she were a kind of rat) and 'assembling shards of diverse cultures' (as if she were a mad archaeologist).[7] There was method, however, to Weil's madness. While political neo-tribalism was threatening to bring Europe down in ruins, she turned her attention to the very cradle of tribalism, religion – whose essence, for her, lay elsewhere

– to see where it had gone astray. Unsurprisingly, her distrust of tribalism, old and new, extended, in spite of the rise of Hitler, to the cause of Zionism. '[She] saw yet another danger', writes Cabaud, 'in the creation of a Jewish state in Palestine: why create a new nationality? We suffer already from the existence of young nations born in the nineteenth century and animated by exacerbated nationalism . . . The existence of an old Jewish tradition in Palestine is the best reason for creating a Jewish homeland elsewhere but in Jerusalem.'[8]

While Weil was scavenging, the armies of Europe were massing, each country priding itself on its exclusive superiority. Simone, however, had never been tempted by this all too natural preference for 'one's own'. With Marx, she had earlier understood that the source of alienated labour did not consist in the fact that capitalists are very bad people, and she now realized, as few others did, that the source of the coming debacle did not lie in the unique perversity of the German people,[9] who could only be stopped by the serendipitous virtue of the French and British.[10] Wittgenstein, once again showing his kinship with Weil, on hearing his student Norman Malcolm declare that the British were too 'civilized' to have been guilty of a bomb plot to assassinate Hitler, responded by breaking off their friendship.

Weil sought, rather, to confront the reality, the 'logic' of force itself as she had in 'On Oppression and Liberty', except now it was the naked force that is the very condition of war, the condition into which all of Europe was descending. As always, her thoughts turned toward ancient Greece. In 'The *Iliad*: Poem of Force', she re-thinks Homer's great epic in a shocking new way. No longer does the display of competing images of the heroism and glory of great souls from the Bronze Age take centre stage. Achilles broods while Hector rages, but these are but footnotes to what Weil sees as the central theme, that 'force is that which makes a thing of anybody who comes under its sway'.[11] It is this message, for Weil, that cuts through the reader like a knife. If the soul, as she puts it, 'is the human being considered as having a value in himself',[12] then in war, the theatre of force, the soul is a mere bystander. In war, as in life, the soul, 'the infinite which is in man', is paradoxically 'at the mercy of a little piece of iron'.[13] The lesson to be learned from Homer, says Weil, is that the human race 'is not divided between the vanquished, the slaves, the suppliants on the one hand, and conquerors and masters on the other. No single man is to be found who is not, at some time, forced to bow beneath might.'[14] Appearances notwithstanding, the moral of Homer's story is not that each glorious hero has his time in the sun, but that the true God is just – he is equitable, as geometry is – and he hands out 'retribution, of a geometric strictness, which punishes automatic - ally the abuse of strength'.[15]

A startling interpretation of Homer. But there is more. 'The Gospels', says Weil, as we saw earlier, 'are the last and most marvel - ous expression of Greek genius, as the *Iliad* is its first expression.'[16] What comes next, however, has set alarm bells off. In contrast to the Gospels, Weil announced, 'the Romans and the Hebrews both believed themselves exempt from the common misery of man, the Romans by being chosen by destiny to be the rulers of the world, the Hebrews [the 'Chosen People'] by the favor of their God'.[17] For Weil, with rare but important exceptions like the Book of Job,[18] 'the Hebrews saw a trace of sin in all affliction and therefore a legitimate motive for despising it'.[19] Whereas, as she had put it in her lectures, 'the Christian revolution consisted in not despising the weak',[20] in ancient Israel, as in Rome, suffering and persecution were viewed as signs of God's disfavour, which serve as 'a legiti - mate motive for despising' those on whom history has trampled. Christianity for Weil not only refuses to look down on the weak, but 'does not seek a supernatural remedy for suffering, but a super- natural use of suffering'.[21] From blows man can only be protected by armour – an 'armor of lies'[22] – whereas the grace that springs from God 'cannot prevent wounds', but 'can prevent these blows from corrupting the soul'.[23]

For some, these 'rantings against Judaism' indicate that this 'spiritual freelancer' had turned into an anti-Semite whose 'skewed reading of the Old Testament' betrayed in equal parts her Jewish self-hatred and her 'ignorance of Judaism'.[24] The question becomes psychological – a matter of hand-wringing and finger-pointing – to account for her prejudice, not philosophical, to evaluate her ideas. Yet the investigation of her thought repays with interest the effort that is demanded. We need to remind ourselves that the Old and New Testaments[25] are, after all, among other things, symbolic systems, texts that cry out for inner, 'hermeneutic' evaluation, and to then ask the question of whether such an evaluation sheds any light on what Weil was up to in the con - cluding sections of her essay on the *Iliad*. It does. If we turn to Elaine Scarry's monumental study, *The Body in Pain: The Making and Unmaking of the World*,[26] a very different picture emerges of the significance of Weil's theology. (Scarry herself, it should be noted, draws attention to Weil's essay.)

Weil focuses on the significance of man's embodied state, which makes him subject to the rule of force, to the subjugation of pain, including the pain of dying. In turn, one of Scarry's primary theses is that 'the relation between man and God [in the Old Testament] becomes a power relation based on the fact that one has a body and the other does not, a relation that is itself radically revised in the Christian scripture where the moral distance between man and God is as great as in the Old Testament but no longer depends on a discrepancy in embodiedness.'[27] To have a body is to be, essentially, a victim, to be other than God. 'God confirms his existence before humanity', says Scarry, 'in the bodies of human beings themselves rather than in any materialization of Himself'.[28] That is why, 'in the Hebraic scriptures . . . God's most intimate contact with humanity . . . [is] mediated by the weapon, [whereas] in the Christian tradition it is mediated by Jesus . . . Hence . . . it is the weapon (not Jehovah) that Jesus replaces.'[29] And thus, although 'in the New [Testament, as in the Old] the human body substantiates the existence of God . . . rather than that bodily verification occurring in the bodily alteration of pain, it occurs in the bodily alteration of sensory apprehension . . . in the hand of a woman touching Jesus, not in the thousands cut and killed in the desert beneath Horeb'.[30]

In the Old Testament, God wounds man; in the New, man wounds God. Scarry is drawing attention to the same symbolic inversion addressed by Weil. It is Scarry, not Weil, who writes that 'in the Old Testament scenes of hurt, Jehovah enters sentience by producing pain; Jesus . . . enters . . . by healing . . . by himself becoming the object of touch'.[31] True, unlike Weil, who reads all this, as she does everything, as a morality tale, Scarry's theme is the role of embodiment and disembodiment in man's 'making' and 'unmaking' of his world, and his God; yet if there is force to her reasoning, the 'symbolic facts' on which Weil bases her asymmetric treatment of the two Testaments cannot be dismissed as mere illusions dreamed up by her feverish anti-Semitic imagination. Faced with a new dawn of nations rising up to claim their birthright as the 'Chosen People' – chosen by fate or history or God – Weil, the philosopher, is searching not for a means to destroy them, but for the very meaning of destruction, of force and its relationship to 'Chosenness'. 'The *Iliad*, Poem of Force' is a first step in that quest.

There will be others. She will revisit the lost world of the medieval Cathars, the Albigensians of Languedoc, in southern France, where Greek and Christian ideas were married (and the Old Testament excluded), only to be crushed in the thirteenth century by kings and crusaders – an oasis of idealism floating in the desert of history (or in Weil's words, one of those 'historical atolls of the living past left upon the surface of the earth'[32]). She will visit Venice in its prime, threatened with annihilation, yet saved (by its beauty), in her imagination, in her play, *Venice is Saved*.[33] The past for her is not dead. She is turning to history, real and imagined, 'scavenging' through time as if it were space.

She is turning back to history; but Hitler is making it. He annexes Austria, he moves into the Sudetenland, he takes Prague, he attacks Poland. It is 3 September 1939; finally, the war is on. Nations are crumbling, but the French grasp at straws, at the fantasy of the Maginot line. Yet while France is fighting the last war, Hitler has invented a new one, and there is no match for his Panzers, no stopping the Blitzkrieg. The French are retreating at unbelievable speed. 13 June 1940: guns are heard in the distance. Simone and her parents are shopping when the news comes that Paris is declared an open city. They catch the last train south and begin their flight. At each stop Simone needs to be convinced not to go back. At Nevers, they awake to see Panzers rumbling down city streets. Simone decides that henceforth the floor will be her only bed. Her shame at her pacifism, now dead, her reluctance to fight, is just beginning. Not the harm she is now suffering, but the harm caused by her opposition to war is what lacerates her.

It is the same with her country. The guilt of French colonialism chokes her. Even as France is invaded, as Panzers roll through Paris, she cannot let go the harm done not *to* but *by* her country. 'A great day for Indo-China', she enters into her notebook – and opens the door to infamy. Once again, it seems, she is showing her true colours. For Jeffrey Mehlman in *Émigré New York*,[34] it is too much. 'She was a Jew', he writes, 'who, in that conflict, had at the outset switched sides.' He searches for a comparison and finds it in Jacques Vergès, the lawyer who will defend Klaus Barbie, the Butcher of Lyon. 'Weil's searing line on the occasion of the Nazi entry into Paris', says Mehlman, 'deserves to be paired with the half-Vietnamese Vergès' quip during the Barbie trial to the effect that his mother did not have to wear a yellow star because she was yellow from head to toe.'

Had Weil really 'switched sides'? Who, we must ask, is affixing a star on whom? What does it mean, after all, to be a patriot, to love 'one's own'? In *The Need for Roots*, written during her final days, Weil will stress that 'to be rooted is perhaps the most important and least recognized need of the human soul'.[35] The harm that springs from rootlessness is the bane of modern civilization. 'Whoever is uprooted, himself uproots others.'[36] Though she has spent a lifetime raging against 'the collective', that 'great beast' of society that Plato warns us against in the *Republic*, she acknowledges at the same time that 'we have no other life, no living sap, than the treasures stored up from the past',[37] and the collectivity is 'the sole agency for preserving [these] spiritual treasures accumulated by the dead.'[38]

Does patriotism, however, the love of one's own, have limits? 'Present day patriotism', she writes, 'consists in an equation between absolute good and a collectivity . . . a given territorial area, namely France.'[39] Patriotism, a necessity, leads almost irresistibly to an overvaluation of our own. The great logician Gottlob Frege, in his political diaries, puts his finger on an ugly truth: '[A] prejudice is necessary for patriotism. He who finds it necessary to conduct an unbiased examination of all people to make up his mind as to who is best knows no true patriotism.'[40] The same could be said of a parent's love. *The familiar* is not *the good*. Yet as human beings, we cannot but cling to the familiar. In effect, as Plato says in the *Republic*, we must live a lie – albeit a 'noble' one, if things are set up right.

Let's recall how Plato got there. At 375–6 of the *Republic*, Socrates suggests that the 'guardians' of his ideal state should resemble pedigree dogs which are simultaneously spirited and gentle. Like philosophers, he says, they are attracted to what they know, their owners, and hostile to what is strange. He's lying, of course. Philosophers love *the good*, while guard dogs are attached to *the familiar*. They substitute acquaintance for knowledge; a familiar Nazi, to them, is as good as the Good. On a deeper level, however, Socrates' lie hides the truth. The Republic, which is founded on the 'vertical', the good, cannot survive without the 'horizontal', the familiar. The glue that makes 'one out of many' cannot dispense with familiarity. To be unbiased toward 'one's own' is not to know patriotism. As Frege said, a prejudice is necessary. Political, hence human, life is founded on a lie. We cannot eliminate it; we can only make it 'noble'.

The historical Socrates, it should be recalled, though he stressed in the *Apology* the difference, as Weil would put it, between Athens and God, also insisted in the *Crito* that a country will not long survive unless its citizens are willing to make the ultimate sacrifice. He would no doubt have agreed with Weil that one is not only permitted but obliged to love 'one's own' – but not *absolutely*. Only an absolute object can sustain an absolute love. Recall – as Weil does not – Abraham being asked by God to sacrifice Isaac. You must love your own, but you must not, as it were, 'make a religion' out of it.

'A nation', writes Weil, 'cannot be the object of supernatural [i.e. absolute] love. It has no soul.'[41] Yet there is no limit to what it asks of us: 'the essence of the contradiction inherent in patriotism is that one's country is something limited whose demands are unlimited.'[42] Weil is agreeing with Socrates that true patriotism demands, if the situation calls for it, the ultimate sacrifice, since 'not to be resolved to give it everything in case of need is to abandon it entirely, for its preservation cannot be assured at any lesser price'.[43] Yet just for this reason, patriotism, if unchecked, leads naturally to idolatry, to the temptation to believe that something whose demands are unlimited is itself unlimited, whereas 'never in this world can there be any dimensional equality between an obligation and its subject. The obligation is unlimited. Its subject is not.'[44]

But why, then, is patriotism itself necessary? In the opening sections of *The Need for Roots* Weil, echoing Socrates in the *Crito*, makes the point that 'we owe respect to a collectivity, of whatever kind – country, family, or any other – not for itself, but because it is food for a certain number of human souls', and that 'the food which a collectivity supplies . . . has no equivalent in the entire universe'.[45] Yet is this not true of all collectivities? Why is one's own special? Precisely because it is one's own. It is here that Weil introduces what she calls 'the need for roots', what we have been speaking of as the importance of the familiar. 'Just as there are . . . certain types of soil for certain plants', she writes, 'so there is a certain part of the soul in every one . . . which can only exist in a national setting and disappears when a country is destroyed.'[46] And yet it is necessary to remind oneself that, 'more than one nation exists on the earth's surface. Ours is unique. But each of the others, considered by itself and with affection, is unique in the same degree.'[47]

It is a question of perspective. Whatever is 'one's own' – country, family, religion, self – will, unless some other force intervenes, always assume its natural position as the centre of the world. The familiar masquerades as the good. Yet this is an illusion of perspective, since 'nothing *in* the world is the centre of the world; . . . that centre . . . lies *outside*'.[48] It is 'God, [who], outside the universe, is at the same time its centre, [even though] each man imagines he is situated in the centre'.[49] In her remark that it was 'a great day for Indo-China', Weil was herself providing that contrary force, correcting the distortions attendant on (an overly) natural perspective. It is unsurprising, then, that a sharp-eyed political observer like Conor Cruise O'Brien should note that Weil's political thought is most striking when it deals with 'basic political bonding . . . in tribe, nation, state – and . . . the original sin of that bonding, the notion of the inherent superiority of the entity constituted by it.' Indeed, he concludes that 'in her consistent witness against that concept . . . lies the great and permanent value of Simone Weil's political writing.'[50]

No one, however, has brought out more forcefully the significance of Weil's scandalous comment on Indo-China than David Rieff in 'European Time'.[51] He acknowledges how shocking it was that Weil 'chose that instant of catastrophe to stand off at such a remove from her own interests', and how tempting it is to see this as 'an act of self-hatred (Jewish, French, European all at once)', adding, correctly, that what makes this particularly tempting is the tendency to tie a woman's ideas to her biography. Yet 'the truth is that Weil was stunningly, self-evidently right'.[52] The French colonial empire – which for generations had rained terror onto 'those yellow from head to toe' – would not long survive the fall of France. Thus 'the Vietnamese had every reason to welcome a French defeat . . . and Simone Weil's intuition was borne out. The battle of Dien-bienphu had been lost that morning the Panzers rolled down the Champs-Elysées. As is so often the case, a quarrel between land-lords is nothing but good news for the tenants.'[53]

None of this, of course, alters the fact that that was also a tragic day for France, in particular for the Jews of France. Weil is not denying this, but rather attempting that impartiality, that 'geometrical' evenness of distribution that she attributes to the divine in us. There is nevertheless a feeling, says Rieff, 'that there is something immoral about Weil's impartiality. Perhaps they are right.'[54] And indeed, 'it would have been preposterous to hear Weil's remark from General de Gaulle or from the Chief Rabbi of Paris, whose obligations were to their own constituencies, and . . . to their own time', yet for Weil, a philosopher, who has no constituency, 'it was precisely the right remark . . . to make. That was her job, just as de Gaulle's was war and the Chief Rabbi's the welfare of his people.'[55] There is a sense, Rieff reminds us, in which 'different people are occupying the same space but living through different historical epochs.' Mehlman misses just this when he derides Weil for 'lamenting a holocaust of sorts . . . but it was the holocaust of the 210 Catharist faithful who offered themselves up on the stake at Montségur some seven hundred years earlier'.[56] Our bodies may occupy co-ordinate positions, but that does not prevent our minds from fixing on different eras. 'In one ruthless, Olympian sentence', says Rieff, 'Weil reminded us that the history we in the West care about . . . is neither the history of everywhere nor of everyone.'[57] We must remember, he insists, that 'an event that for us is cause for mourning may be celebrated by other people every bit as decent as us'.[58] The centre, indeed, lies elsewhere. That 'European Time' is not universal is brought out clearly by Weil in *The Need for Roots*,[59] where she remarks that 'it is said that God had sent Christopher Columbus to America in order that a few centuries later there should be a nation capable of defeating Hitler'. European time. 'God, apparently, also despises coloured races: the wholesale extermination of native American peoples in the sixteenth century seemed to him a small price to pay if it meant the salvation of Europeans in the twentieth.'

A great day for Indo-China: with her country collapsed, with her recriminations about her failure to foresee the deluge, Weil did not allow the war to blind her by patriotism. Yet her own family remained in peril. Hearing that there would be an Unoccupied Zone, they fled to Vichy, thence to Marseilles, where for the next eighteen months they would set up a second life. They found a place to live on rue de Catalans, near the Old Port, with a view of the ocean, and Simone found a place to work – at *Cahiers du Sud*, a liberal journal founded by filmmaker Marcel Pagnol – where her essay on the *Iliad* and two others on the Albigensians were soon accepted for publication.

Also published was a review by her of Max Planck's *Introduction to Physics*, which gives an idea of the depth of her intellect, the breadth of her interests. Preoccupied with Marx and Homer, not to say with Nazis, her interest in the mathematical sciences remained strong. In her review she takes the father of quantum mechanics to task for introducing discontinuity into fundamental physics.[60] She accuses him of an excessive emphasis on 'convenience of calculation', and especially of an over-reliance on algebra. '[A]lgebra', she writes, 'puts everything on the same plane . . . It is quite flat; the third dimension of thought is absent from it.'[61] In lines later published in *Gravity and Grace* she makes a more sweeping pronouncement: 'Money, mechanization, algebra. The three monsters of contemporary civilization . . . Algebra and money are essentially levelers, the first intellectually, the second, effectively.'[62]

Though she is not her brother, there is nothing amateurish about her remarks. René Thom, the great French geometer, himself took exception to the famous maxim by Leopold Kronecker that 'God created the integers; man made the rest.' For Thom, 'this maxim, spoken by the algebraist Kronecker, reveals more about his past as a banker who grew rich through monetary speculation than about his philosophical insight . . . [On the contrary] the geometrical continuum is the primordial entity. . . . [E]ven in mathematics, quality subsists, and resists all reduction to sets.'[63] Thom's words could easily have been uttered by Weil. A pity they never met. With Weil's concerns about discontinuity in physics, she would have been intrigued by Thom, the inventor of cata - strophe theory – which explains how discontinuity can arise out of continuity.

Though she found time for mathematics, however, Weil could not escape the political reality engulfing her. Excluded from teaching by the new racial laws of Vichy, she sent a letter to the Minister of Education dripping with sarcasm. It focused (to the dismay of her critics) not on the discrimination itself but on the fact that 'I don't know the definition of the word Jew.' It was, apparently, not part of her education. She received no clarification. In a second letter, this time to the Commissioner of Jewish Affairs, she would pour ridicule on the law itself and declare that, 'I look on the statute on

Jews as generally unjust and absurd.'[64] In spite of this, she has been severely taken to task for not simply accepting the label of being a Jew out of 'solidarity' with 'her people'. Yet, 'why would you want to read the letter', notes Jacques Cabaud,[65] correctly, 'as if it were saying, "Too bad for the Jews! I'm not one"?' Weil was attempting, rather, a reductio ad absurdum of the government's new statute. Moreover, 'why reproach Simone Weil for having lacked heroism in this case, when she is soon to risk her life distributing [anti-government] literature, for which one of her fellow distributors was sent to Auschwitz?'

What provoked yet more outrage from Weil was the fact that thousands of immigrant Indo-Chinese labourers were being held in dreadful lockup and forced to work in munitions factories. The 'great day for Indo-China' had not yet borne fruit. She sent a fierce letter to the American ambassador to Vichy and made certain that most of her food coupons found their way into the hands of the imprisoned workers. To political suspects rounded up by Vichy she sent care packets. She joined the Resistance, such as it was at that time, and was assigned to a group – a group, unfortunately, infiltrated by informers. Three times she was visited by the Vichy police, who arrested and interrogated her. Each time she went armed with the *Iliad*, without which she never left home. The interrogations, which never fazed her, came to naught, but the frustrated police threatened to throw the 'bitch' in with the whores – whom Weil said she would be happy to get to know better. And indeed, as we have seen, she did have a lifelong interest in and sympathy for prostitutes. But not for their clients. 'She told me one day', said Thibon, 'that she would refuse to shake hands with any man whom she knew to frequent the houses of prostitutes.'[66]

Later, she came into contact with a schoolteacher, Malou David, who worked for the clandestine anti-Vichy publication *Cahiers du Témoignage Chrétien*. Soon Weil was in charge of its distribution in Marseilles. This time, she did not cross paths with the police,

Gustave Thibon, with Weil's biographer, Jacques Cabaud.

but she did brush up against a far worse fate when she dropped an entire suitcase filled with Resistance papers which scattered across the sidewalk. Luckily, her clumsiness was matched by her sangfroid as she calmly retrieved the documents.

Her wish to get to know prostitutes was exceeded by her desire to understand the ways of the Catholic Church, on the threshold of which she was forever poised. To her good fortune – if not to his – she came into contact with Father Perrin, a young Dominican priest with a strong social conscience, and a sympathetic Hebraist. She confided to him the stumbling blocks on her path to baptism. That one of these was her hostility to the Hebrew Bible came as a rude shock to the gentle Hebrew scholar, who was elsewhere occupied promoting Jewish–Christian relations. It came as no less of a surprise to the monk Dom Clémont Jacob, whom she later confronted in her attempt, yet again, to discover if the obstacles to her being baptized could be overcome. Was it permitted to believe, as Weil did, that Jesus was not the only incarnation of God? (Why not Osiris or Krishna?) Could 'pagans' or contemporary non-Christians receive the divine light as well as Christians? Could one disagree about the fate of unbaptized infants? She had dozens of questions, but he had only one answer. Her hopes for the possibility of baptism, always faint, began to flicker.

Father Perrin, however, though equally sceptical was more sympathetic. Acceding to Weil's request to find a way to engage in the most demanding of farm labours, he put her in touch with his friend, Gustave Thibon, a Catholic philosopher of distinctly conservative bent – he was a speech writer for Marshal Pétain – who had a farm in Saint-Marcel-d'Ardèche, north of Marseilles. Cautious at first, Thibon soon embraced her, in spite of, or perhaps because of, their great differences. One of his favourites, Victor Hugo, she declared a 'sonorous imbecile'. His inclination toward Nietzsche, shared by her brother, André, was matched by her revulsion. And his defence of Vichy fell on deaf ears.

On a deeper level, however, they were kindred spirits, and spent countless hours discussing God and philosophy. At night, sitting outside, she read Plato's *Phaedo* with him in the original Greek. Finding his house too comfortable, she was happy to abide in a ramshackle little hut a few miles away, with her sleeping bag on a pile of pine needles and a little desk in the corner. In spite of her frailty she proved an indefatigable worker, rising at 5 am to milk the cows, putting out fodder for the cattle, joining in with the housework. She took meals with the family, yet 'to make her accept an egg was no easy task'.[67] Accompanied everywhere by her clumsiness, she had adapted to it as to an old friend. 'The way she held the plates when washing up, which was as careful as it was unnatural, was enough to set me off in fits of irresistible laughter.'[68] Her

The dilapidated house at Saint-Marcel-d'Ardèche in which Weil lived during August and September 1941 while working as a farmhand with Gustave Thibon.

In Marseilles with writer and translator Jean Lambert, spring 1941.

self-deprecating humour disarmed her friend. She acknowledged, as we saw earlier, that smoking was her 'Achilles' heel'. Watching her counting out the wages she had earned with back-breaking labour, Thibon commented that he had 'no illusions about the destiny of this sum', to which the response came, 'but I shall certainly *also* buy some books!'[69]

Thibon was not a particularly modest man, but he had no illusions about his special guest: 'I am quite aware that the mere fact of knowing and loving someone who is superior to oneself necessarily creates tension; nothing is more likely to produce storms than differences of altitude.' Simone, it might be said, had the friends she deserved. For herself, however, her '"phenomenal self"', to use the language of Kant . . . she had the greatest contempt . . . [H]er humility in this realm bordered on an inferiority complex.'[70] Yet, in the end, she acknowledged that even she might have served a divine purpose: 'It may be that God has made use of me to draw you a little nearer. He is not hard to please in his choice of tools. He makes a practice of the recovery of refuse.'[71] Nevertheless, she

In Marseilles, winter 1941–2.

could not help adding that 'I am not a person with whom it is advisable to link one's fate.'[72]

Though he could not break the shell in which she had imprisoned herself –or at least its 'phenomenal' aspect – he did succeed in penetrating some of the thoughts she shared with him with complete and unguarded generosity. She was not the host who puts out the cheapest wine. Human love, she said, is born from a chance meeting. It is not unconditional. 'A woman thinks she is loved for herself, but what is the [phenomenal] self but a tissue of ephemeral appearances? If the lover owned to her, "I love you for your beauty, or your intelligence, and my love will therefore last as long as this beauty or this intelligence . . ." she would feel herself penetrated with the coldness of death. Yet that is the truth of human love.'[73] Her conclusion: 'It is untrue to say that love is stronger than death; death is stronger.'

But she is speaking here of human love. To the unconditioned object, there belongs unconditional love. 'Simone Weil is, before all things', says Thibon, 'a guide on the road leading the soul to God . . . [She is giving] *advice to travelers*. The first advice she gives is: not to bring luggage . . .'.[74] The Church, by contrast, is a thing of this world, and 'she reproached it for being . . . a social and totalitarian organism, modeled on imperial Rome . . . which proclaimed that there was no salvation outside itself and which anathematized those who rejected its authority.'[75] Her attack was relentless; nothing Thibon said could abate it: 'How many times did she not tell me that Catholic totalitarianism was, in a sense, infinitely worse than that of men like Hitler or Stalin, since it condemned all refractory spirits to eternal torture whereas the tyranny of dictators did at least cease on death.'[76]

When not scolding the Church, Weil continued to throw herself into her labours. Thibon secured her a place at other farms where she took part in the grape harvest, spending eight hours a day at the vineyards. She was often too tired to keep standing, and so continued to pick grapes lying down. In addition she milked cows at dawn, peeled vegetables and, as always, helped the local children with their homework. As always, too, her meagre diet alarmed her hosts who 'had to watch her like a hawk' lest she confine her meals to the occasional onion or tomato. Somehow, she found time to master Sanskrit, adding yet another ancient language to her repertoire, and to study the Upanishads. Her French exile had not been wasted.

Finally, after a year and a half in Marseilles, the family acquires exit visas to the United States. They are booked on a cargo boat, the ss *Maréchal Lyautey*, bound for Casablanca, to await there their voyage to New York. She bids farewell to Father Perrin, and hands over notebooks that will become the basis for *Waiting for God*. To Thibon she gives, almost absentmindedly, twelve large notebooks, selections from which he will later publish as *Gravity and Grace*. In Casablanca she will work feverishly on what will become part of *Intimations of Christianity Among the Ancient Greeks*. She tells Thibon not to be sad. He must love the distance that will soon come between them, since 'those who do not love each other cannot be separated'.[77]

6

A Difference between France and God

Joan of Arc's popularity during the past quarter-century was not an altogether healthy business; it was a convenient way of forgetting that there is a difference between France and God.
Simone Weil

In Casablanca, where Humphrey Bogart had gone for the waters, the Weils, together with 900 others (mainly Jews), spent seventeen days in the refugee camp of Aïn-Seba. Simone kidnapped one of the few available chairs, sat down, and never stopped writing. At night she slept on the ground, this time with all the others. At dawn she was fascinated by the sight, new to her eyes, of the tallith and phylacteries of the Polish rabbis in the garden, swaying back and forth while saying their prayers. She took time to write to Perrin, her friendship, she said, demanding that she gently rebuke him for his excessive 'attachment to the Church as to an earthly fatherland'.[1] As for herself, she confided that her way of being a Christian must forever be foreign to him; she was 'kept outside the Church' by her 'love of those things which are outside visible Christianity' – ancient Greece, India, the 'implicit love of God' hidden in the hearts of those who do not belong to any church.

Finally, on 7 June 1942, they took leave for the United States on the Portuguese ship *Serpa Pinto*. During their month at sea, Simone, the raven, with her black cape covering her body from head to toe, kept apart from the cabin passengers who, unlike her, had no trouble enjoying the benefits denied those in steerage. She attended only to a young child who had a mental disability (such children had always had a special place in her heart) and to a young man, Jacques Kaplan ('*mon petit Jacques*'), who had volunteered to take care of the refugee children in the hold. He found her 'very pleasant, very protective, very sarcastic'.[2] The *Serpa Pinto* docked in New York Harbor on 8 July. Simone had never liked America, and her brief stay in New York City was not likely to change her mind. It was a country, she thought, that lacked historical consciousness. 'We have only to look at the United States', she wrote later, 'to see what it is to have a people deprived of the time-dimension.'[3] Earlier, she had written to her brother from Marseilles that the hospitality of Americans 'is a purely philanthropic matter, and it is repugnant to me to be the object of philanthropy'. In typical fashion, she declared that 'it is more flattering . . . to be the object of persecution.'[4] Her great compatriot Baudelaire would have agreed.[5]

Her distrust of the country she had just entered was exacerbated by her immediate realization that she had made a mistake in forsaking Marseilles, assuming it would be easy to move on from New York to London and thence to join the French Resistance. It was not only not easy, it was nearly impossible. She was devastated. 'I feel like a deserter', she wrote in desperation to someone she'd heard on the radio who she thought could help: 'My life has no value to me as long as Paris . . . is subject to German domination.'[6] To her friend, Maurice Schumann, with whom she had sat side by side in Alain's classes and who was now in London with the Free French, she wrote: 'I beg you to get me over to London. Don't let me die of grief here.'[7] To him, to the philosopher Jacques Maritain, now also in America, and to anyone else she could think of, she pleaded to be given a chance to implement her plan, hatched earlier, of sending nurses on a suicidal mission to the front lines, to give emergency aid and, more importantly, spiritual support

A contemporary photo of Simone's niece Sylvie Weil.

to the soldiers (not least, by reminding them for whom they were fighting). As André wrote to her, however, from Haverford College, where he was being shamefully underemployed, it was no easy business crossing the dangerous Atlantic, which was swarming with U-boats. Even getting permission to step into a boat was difficult for a French citizen, for whom authorization was required from the Americans, the British and the Free French. Simone was a rat caught in a trap of her own making.

At Haverford on the edge of Philadelphia, her brother was caught in a different kind of trap. On arriving in America, André, who had already made distinguished contributions to mathematics for which he had acquired international fame, had been informed by the Rockefeller Foundation that with his 'lack of experience in American teaching methods',[8] he would do well to accept a one-year position as, in effect, an instructor at Haverford College, for which the Foundation would pay his salary. The following year, 1942–3, he fared even worse, ending up at 'a second-rate engineering school attached to Bethlehem Steel'.[9] He had applied for a job in the Midwest, only to be informed he had no chance, since 'you're Jewish, you're a foreigner, and you're too good a mathematician for these people'.[10] He would soon send a letter to his friend, Hermann Weyl, at Princeton's Institute for Advanced Study, declaring his frustration: 'Prostitution consists in diverting something of high value to base uses for mercenary reasons; this is what I have been doing these two years.'[11]

On a personal level, however, there was good news. He had been married a few years earlier, to his mother's great displeasure, to Eveline, an attractive divorcée. Raised Catholic, with a son, Alain, from a previous marriage, she now bore him a daughter, Sylvie. Fortunately, said André, though they lived in Bethlehem, she was born not there but nearby, in Fountain Hill, since '"Weil, born in Bethlehem," would have seemed a bit conspicuous to her, especially if she had been a boy.'[12] Still, they acquired the services of '[a] good person named Mary . . . [from] Nazareth,[13] to assist Eveline. Simone, too, came to their assistance – or so she thought – by giving Sylvie her bottle (with surprising skill) and by urging the young parents to have their daughter baptized. 'All baptism meant to me was a few drops of water on a baby's head', wrote André, and so 'it didn't take much to persuade me.' Eveline, for her part, who 'still felt ties to her childhood religion . . . [and] often went to mass [accompanied by her husband]', was also untroubled. It seems not to have occurred to anyone that Sylvie herself might, in time, have her own objections. She did.

In her memoirs, Sylvie Weil writes of reading a letter from her aunt in which she says that in light of 'more or less anti-Semitic legislation . . . it would be good for [Sylvie] to enjoy certain advantages, without being cowardly'.[14] How shocked would Simone have been to have seen what comes next: 'This sentence', writes her niece, 'drove me nuts. It seemed disgraceful, to my aunt and to me . . . There was [apparently] in her a sort of cowardice,[15] precisely, which she didn't hesitate to attribute to me. This baptism that she

Passport photo of Weil, New York, October/November, 1942.

refused for herself, she tosses at me, while herself staying pure.'[16] And then the clincher: 'She keeps heroism for herself.' True, indeed. And yet, is it not this way with all heroes? Does not the soldier who chooses to fall on a grenade to save his comrade deny him the chance to become a hero? And what about the sacrifice at Golgotha? Simone herself came close to echoing Sylvie's lament when she said that she 'envied' Christ on the cross. Unfortunately for her, the job was already taken.

Heroes and cowards aside, did it occur to Simone that her niece might have returned to her ancestors? 'How mistaken she was about what I would become', writes Sylvie.[17] 'For several years, I studied Hebrew seriously, plunging into the Judaism . . . that Simone had so obstinately refused to acquaint herself with . . . I became passionate about . . . Rashi [the great medieval Talmudist].' Yet did not Simone, for her part, plunge into the Christianity that Sylvie has 'so obstinately refused to acquaint herself with' – assuming she is not as intimately acquainted with St John of the Cross as she is with Rashi. If Simone can be accused of 'ignoring' the religion of her ancestors, cannot Sylvie be accused of 'ignoring' the religion not just of her aunt, but of her mother, Eveline, raised Catholic, and of Alain, the son from Eveline's first marriage, who, with Simone's assistance, received first communion from Father Couturier, a distinguished French Dominican? And yet a kinship remains. Like Simone, with her devotion to the medieval civilization of the Cathars of Languedoc, Sylvie has chosen to spend her time in the company of Rashi, also in the Middle Ages – indeed, in the same century, the twelfth, where her aunt resided. The apple, after all, did not fall so very far from the tree.

Back in New York City, Simone did not feel like a hero so much as a rat. The hole into which she had retreated was an apartment located on the Upper West side, at 549 Riverside Drive, between 123rd and 124th Streets. She explored Harlem and attended daily Mass at the Franciscan Church of Corpus Christi, on 121st Street. She liked the fact that the service was in English, believing the tradition of Latin to be yet another bad legacy from Rome. Occasionally, she went to a small synagogue of Ethiopian Jews, while every Sunday she attended services at a Baptist church in Harlem, the only white member of the congregation. She especially loved the pastor's fervour and the dancing that broke out afterwards, which she described as 'a true and moving expression of faith'.[18] 'She got in touch with the black girls', notes Father Perrin, 'and invited them to her home.'[19] Indeed, a friend of hers remarked that 'it is certain that had she stayed in New York, she would have become black'.[20]

She continued her study of pre-Christian myths, this time exploring the folk stories of Native Americans. At the Public Library she looked into the possibility of a relationship between Irish and ancient Greek mythologies. She continued to harass any priest she could lay hands on with her questions about Church dogma. She never abandoned her quest, by now quixotic, to find out if there was some way she could hold on to her 'heresies' and still join the fold. In the end, in a long letter to Father Couturier – published posthumously as a small book, *Letter to a Priest* – that ran to 32 large manuscript pages filled with her tiny handwriting, she announced 35 'heretical propositions' of whose truth she was not fully convinced, but which at the same time she believed 'it is not legitimate to deny . . . categorically'.[21] These included the proposition that God was no less present in pre-Christian myths than in Christianity, and that the doctrine of *anathama sit*, by which the Church casts out heretics, could be compared to the Nazis. And she expressed, yet again, her outrage over (what she took to be) Church doctrine on unbaptized infants.[22]

Of special note is what she singled out as a kind of fundamental axiom, that 'the essential truth concerning God[23] is that He is Good'.[24] From this axiom, a crucial theorem immediately follows: 'To believe that God can order men to commit the most atrocious acts of injustice and cruelty is the greatest mistake it is possible to make with regard to Him.'[25] She had rediscovered a conclusion reached long ago by her beloved Plato in his dialogue, *The Euthyphro*. To test Euthyphro's proposed definition of piety as what the gods (all the gods, i.e. in effect, God) approve of – or love or command – Socrates poses a question that still resonates down the centuries: is something good *because God commands it*, or does God command it *because it is good*? Weil, like Socrates, affirms the latter. If this is correct, however, what is one to make of those passages in the Bible, in particular, the Hebrew Bible, in which God appears to order what can only be described as massacres?

For Weil, the answer is obvious: we must reject them. She is in good company. In a discussion of how to interpret the Bible, Immanuel Kant considers a troubling text: 'Take Psalm 59, vv. 1–16, where we find a prayer for revenge that borders on the horrific. Michaelis (*Ethics*, Part II, p. 202) approves of this prayer and adds: "The Psalms are inspired; if they pray for revenge, then it cannot be wrong. We should not have a holier morality than the Bible."

I pause here at this last statement and ask whether morality must be interpreted in accordance with the Bible, or the Bible, on the contrary, in accordance with morality.'[26] Kant, for whom only the latter is acceptable, is thus on the side of the *Euthyphro*.

But the other side, too, does not lack support. In a discussion with Moritz Schlick on the nature of ethics, Wittgenstein parts company with his colleague's choice of Plato: 'I think [the following] conception [of the essence of the good] is the deeper one: Good is what God orders. For this cuts off the path to any and every explanation of 'why' it is good, while the second conception is precisely the superficial, the rationalistic one'.[27] The contemporary Jewish philosopher Michael Wyschogrod agrees with Wittgenstein's conclusion, if not his reasoning. He declares outright that '[Jewish ethics] is not the ethics of the *Euthyphro* of Plato.'[28] He is contradicted, however, it should be noted, by the great medieval Jewish philosopher Saadia Gaon, by whose lights 'God does what is rational or just because it is a priori rational or just; it is not rational or just *because* God does it .'[29]

But there are more opponents of Plato. Abraham Heschel, in *God in Search of Man: A Philosophy of Judaism*,[30] declares that he has no use for Plato's dialogue. Yet, if we examine his discussion more keenly, it emerges that he is in fact closer to Plato than to Wittgenstein. True, he begins by saying that 'to the philosopher, the idea of the good is the most exalted idea. But to the Bible the idea of the good is penultimate; it cannot exist without the holy.'[31] He continues, however, by adding that the problem of the dialogue can only arise 'when the gods and the good are considered as two different entities', whereas 'the righteousness of God [i.e. his goodness] is inseparable from his being.' But this conclusion is precisely Plato's, in contrast to Wittgenstein! And it rests on the very distinction Plato is making. Heschel is in effect agreeing with Plato and Weil that *God is essentially good*, that goodness is an inextricable part of his being. That is precisely what makes God,

God. That is, God is God *because* he is essentially good, not: what is good is good *because* it is what God orders; whereas the latter is precisely the view endorsed by Plato's opponent, Wittgenstein.

Heschel, then, does not have to face the question that confronts Wittgenstein: why should we *care* what God orders, if His orders are not founded on goodness? Should we fear his power? This is indeed stressed in parts of the Hebrew Bible, yet Wittgenstein himself, though, as we have seen, he told his friend Drury that he was 'one hundred per cent Hebraic', claimed that 'if I thought of God as another being like myself, outside myself, only infinitely more powerful, then I would regard it as my duty to defy him.'[32] The *Euthyphro*, it seems, has succeeded in driving a wedge not only between Kant and Wittgenstein, but between Wittgenstein and himself.

Simone, clearly, in her theological manifesto was fishing in deep waters, but she could not (try as she might) survive on thought alone. Lonely and desperate, she haunted the Free French headquarters where, fortuitously, she reacquainted herself with Simone Deitz, a converted Catholic whom she had met in Marseilles. 'Will you be my friend?', she asked. Thirsting for a companion, she sought one out and found her – against her own philosophy. 'To wish to escape from solitude is cowardice', she had written. 'To desire friendship is a great fault . . .You would sell your soul for friendship.'[33] Both of them hoping to get to London, they attended a first aid course in Harlem, believing it would be of help. It wasn't. But the friendship did help to improve Simone's miserable diet. Dining often with her friend's family, she would be tricked by Deitz's canny father, who would go out of his way to declaim the superiority of Judaism to the Christian faith; while Weil was preoccupied with launching her counter-reply, he would slip some extra food onto her plate. She never noticed.

Extra portions or not, however, she was pining away, with a broken heart and a guilty conscience. Another friendship – this time her old one with Maurice Schumann – came to the rescue. In mid-September, he sent word that André Philip, from de Gaulle's provisional government, would be visiting New York, and that he was looking forward to enlisting Simone. They met a few weeks later and the deal was sealed. Simone, together with her friend, Simone Deitz, was bound for London. Her anxious parents, for all their pleas, could not join her. 'If I had several lives', she said to them, 'I would have dedicated one of them to you.' It was the first, and the last time she would part with them.

On 10 November 1942 the Swedish cargo ship *Vaalaren* sailed out of New York Harbor in a small convoy, bearing Simone and ten other passengers. Deitz was on another ship. The following day, not five months since Simone had left France, German forces descended on Vichy. With enthusiastic help from the police, they rounded up thousands of Jews. In a 'target rich' environment, Marseilles stood out. In all, 25,000 men, women and children were sent off to concentration camps, their fates sealed. It was the second time Simone Weil had cheated death, first in Spain and now in Marseilles. There would not be a third.

At last Simone was on her way. She was going home. The trip across the Atlantic took two weeks. On deck, under the moonlight, the small group of passengers gathered to hear Simone tell folk tales. Asked why she ate so little, she replied that she would not allow herself to consume more than her compatriots in France were allowed to eat. It was a principle she would (indeed, most likely, could) never violate. Landing at Liverpool, the passengers were transported to a waiting camp. Because of her leftist associations, she was detained for two weeks. Taking advantage of her newly acquired leisure, the former champion rugby player learned to play volleyball. Simone, it seemed, at last, had found a kind of peace.

Yet 'in peace', says Nietzsche, 'the warlike man turns on himself.' Having fled the war in France, Simone was anxious to trade in her newly acquired calm for a chance to engage the enemy. As had happened before, however, in her abortive venture in Spain her attempt to join the Resistance in France was met with extreme prejudice: 'But she is mad!', said de Gaulle. And it was indeed mad, or at least impermissible, for her to be parachuted behind enemy lines if this would have endangered the lives of others. That she would almost certainly have forfeited her own life is something else. Did de Gaulle, however, or anyone else, have the right to deny Simone Weil the opportunity to die for France?[34] Was it an act of mercy to drive her into a self-induced death on foreign soil, brought on by grief and despair, instead of allowing her the violent and heroic act of parachuting into her destiny? Was it merciful to force her to waste her death ('the most precious thing which has been given to man') – to turn a happy warrior into a sad clown?

'[O]ne day when I was detesting you', writes Sylvie Weil to her aunt, 'I ran into a man you knew in London during the war. And the words he used to describe you overwhelmed me. He didn't speak of a comet . . . he spoke of a little young woman who was tired, isolated, invisible, dressed like a poor person, wearing a big beret . . . Your shapeless and overly long skirt swept the floor, ridiculously . . . [T]he poor *trollesse* let herself die of despair because no one took her plan seriously . . . This image of a . . . solitary, rejected Simone . . . hit me hard.'[35] And yet, perhaps this was after all the right death for Simone Weil. 'The martyrs who entered the arena', she wrote, 'singing as they went to face the wild beasts, were not afflicted. Christ was afflicted. He did not die like a martyr. He died like a common criminal, confused with thieves, only a little more ridiculous. For affliction is ridiculous.'[36]

Simone herself realized she had turned into a fool, albeit 'a fool for love', as she would have described Sophocles' Antigone – whose Christ-like death, for Weil, was no less that of a common criminal – with whom she deeply identified (as Marie Cabaud Meaney has emphasized[37]). In her letters home in her final year, Sylvie's 'poor *trollesse*', Bouglé's 'Red Virgin', had chosen for herself, finally, the name of Antigone, Sophocles' divine fool. And Shakespeare's fools were no less on her mind. In London she was deeply affected by a performance of *King Lear*. '[D]o you feel the affinity', she wrote to her mother, 'the essential analogy between these fools and me – in spite of the École and the examination successes and the eulogies of my "intelligence"?'[38]

Without a war to fight, the warlike Weil turned on herself. At the Free French headquarters, she moved heaven and earth in her attempt to put into effect her dramatic plan to form a squadron of front line nurses to tend to the most grievously wounded and to demonstrate to the Nazis – who, she held, to the extreme consternation of her comrades, were far from deficient in courage – that the French, too, could laugh in the face of death. It was at Weil, however, that the French chose to laugh, not least because of her legendary maladroitness, which rendered yet more absurd her alternative plan of being parachuted behind enemy lines to join up with the Resistance. Deitz's attempt to teach her to drive had been abandoned after she had two accidents within ten minutes. Combined with what were taken to be her 'Semitic features', this would put Weil herself and all around her in the gravest danger. In place of a parachute, therefore, she was given a desk – in Hill Street, with Interior Services – her brief was the development of principles on which post-war France would be reconstructed. The result was *The Need for Roots*, her attempt to rebuild France on the basis not of the well-trodden path of human *rights* but of the still unexplored road that points in the direction of our *duties* to our fellow man.

The idea of a redirection from the self-centered concept of rights – so close to the heart of Frenchmen – to the other-directed notion of duties is a powerful one, but though filled with brilliant insights, the book as a whole does not have that organic unity Weil herself believed essential to all great works of art. Part Plato's *Republic*, part French history, part theology, part deontology, the book is a culinary delight without being a complete meal. As is the case with Plato, it is unknown how seriously her detailed political recommendations were intended to be taken. She herself had warned against reading the *Republic* as a literal blueprint for a future society. Concerns about the very real dangers of 'group-think', for example, are one thing, but was she seriously recommending that 'protection of freedom of thought requires that no group should be permitted to express an opinion. For when a group starts having an opinion, it inevitably tends to impose them on its members'?[39]

By contrast, her idea that only something spiritual can compete with the spiritual attractions of totalitarianism has great force, as has her beautiful but dangerous observation about the poetry of violence: 'When men are offered the choice between guns and butter, although they prefer butter so very much more than guns, a mysterious fatality compels them, in spite of themselves, to choose guns. There isn't enough poetry about butter.'[40] Similarly, is there not something remarkable about her insistence, despite her 'supernaturalism', that we must beware of the temptation to give in to a 'spurious mysticism' that would lead us only 'to recognize obligations towards what is not of this world', whereby 'the unfortunate objects of compassion [become] but the raw material for the action, [the] anonymous means whereby one's love of God can be manifested?'[41] Does it not come as a clarion call when she warns us that 'it is only through . . . individual beings on this earth that human love can penetrate to that which lies beyond?'[42]

For five months she laboured in London – *The Need for Roots* being but one of her accomplishments – her guilt at her pre-war pacifism eating into her no less than her anger at being denied the opportunity to die for France. Yet whereas she was never at ease in New York, she felt at home in London. Her dislike for all things American was matched by her affection for the British. She was attracted to their sense of tradition, their 'rootedness'. She found a

FRANCE COMBATTANTE

LAISSEZ-PASSER

No. *1663*   Nom *lle Weil*

Prenoms *Simone*

Grade ou Profession *Redactrice*

Bureau ou Service *C. N. 7*

Londres le *30 Mars 1945*

Le Chef du Service de Sécurité

room in the Notting Hill district, at the home of a cleaning woman, Mrs Francis, whose household was, she said, 'pure Dickens'. The two young Francis children became attached to her. She took a special interest in the younger boy. She tutored him and corrected his homework, which he would leave in the hallway when she was out. She rejected any attempt by Mrs Francis to attend to her own needs. When her landlady would not desist from cleaning her shoes, Simone hid them. She spent most of her days and much of her nights hunched over her desk, where she would sometimes fall asleep, at home or at work, writing. When, on occasion, she ventured out, she enjoyed the scene in the British pubs, so unlike the bars in America, and took in performances of Shakespeare. She explored the streets with her friend Simone Deitz and taught her Tibetan, so that they could read Milarepa together.

But it was Deitz who broke her heart. That her best friend was the one chosen to parachute into France was the final laceration. Her health was already at breaking point. Her life-long reluctance to eat had only intensified during her exile in London, and she had stuck by her decision not to enjoy a greater share of rations than that to which her compatriots in occupied France had been con - fined. Her consumption of tobacco, by contrast, had continued unabated, as had her nearly complete neglect of sleep. Finally, on 15 April 1943, she collapsed. Simone Deitz found her unconscious on the floor of her room. When told she could not avoid going to hospital she burst into tears: 'All is lost!' Into the undefended territory of her body had marched a granular form of tuberculosis, in both lungs. Her long-suffering doctors were immune to the irony of their immediate recommendation: nourishment and rest. She was, they avowed, the worst patient they had ever encountered.

Her true anger, however, was directed against neither her disease nor the doctors trying to fight it. Her full fury was aimed, rather, at the internecine politicking of the Free French, and worse, the continuing rise of an extreme form of French nationalism. For Simone, France was not 'holy France', any more than Germany was home to the 'Master Race'. Yet, as John Hellman notes, 'not only the more "pagan" nationalists such as Maurras and Barrès, but deeply serious Christians such as Bernanos, Léon Bloy, Paul Claudel, and the young Jacques Maritain believed in a special relationship between their beloved country and Divine Providence.'[43] Worse, the Catholic poet Charles Péguy 'produced the most impressive celebration of Joan of Arc's special meaning for France . . . des - cribing God Himself as French.'

Simone Weil could not bear the fact that Saint Joan had been enlisted into this cause. '[Pasteur] serves as a cloak to the idolatry of science', she wrote, 'just as Joan of Arc does to nationalist idolatry.'[44] She was offended by this sullying of the pure name of Saint Joan. 'If one were to look for names which are associated with real purity, one would find very few . . . In French history, would one be able to find another name besides that of Joan of Arc?'[45] All the more reason why one cannot permit such a figure to become a source of idolatry: 'Joan of Arc's popularity during the past quarter century was not an altogether healthy business; it was a convenient way of forgetting that there is a difference between France and God.'[46] Enough was enough.

The Kent countryside seen from Weil's window at Grosvenor Sanatorium, Ashford, where she died in August 1943.

'I cannot have', she finally wrote, 'any direct or indirect or even any very indirect [!] connection with the French Resistance.' 'I am finished', she added, 'broken, beyond any possibility of mending, and that independent of Koch's bacilli. The latter has only taken advantage of my lack of resistance . . . The object may perhaps . . . be only temporarily glued together in such a way as to function for a few more years'.[47] The gluing together, however, would occupy a much briefer span of time. She was placed at first in Middlesex Hospital in London. She refused a private room. But she did ask continually to be transferred to the country, and made certain her little collection of books was packed for the journey: Plato, the

Weil's headstone in Bybrook Cemetery, Ashford.

Bhagavad Gita, St John of the Cross. At last, in mid-August, she was taken to Grosvenor Sanatorium, in bucolic Ashford, Kent. 'What a beautiful room in which to die', she said, on seeing her new accommodation.

On Tuesday, 24 August 1943, a warm summer day, the frail pieces that had never been more than temporarily glued together came apart. She died unbaptized[48] – this 'de-judaised Jewess', as Gabriel Marcel referred to her.[49] As ever, she could not bring herself to embrace the idea of separation – from non-Catholics and Jews no less than unbaptized children. For this she has never been forgiven.

7

Fêtes de la Faim

The eternal part of the soul feeds on hunger.
Simone Weil

Simone Weil's death, provoked by a starvation diet that accelerated her already aggressive tuberculosis, was the final chapter in her life-long war with food. For her, eating was both enemy and weapon. Du Plessix Gray is right to draw attention to the extraordinarily powerful role food, and the images thereof, played in Weil's life and writings. Less convincing is her insistence that this can be 'explained' by invoking the medical condition known as anorexia nervosa. Less convincing still is the suggestion that Weil might have been 'attracted to Christianity because of its obsessive emphasis on food, because of the cannibalistic associations of Holy Communion'.[1] And although it is true that Weil was deeply conflicted about her Jewish ancestry, can one really believe that her self-induced death was an attempt to kill the Jew in her, that she 'might have speeded her death through her loathing for her Jewish body' – not to say, 'her failure to acknowledge the deeply Jewish beauty of her mind'[2] – whatever might be meant by a 'deeply Jewish [as opposed to Methodist?] beauty' of a mind.

It is not that anorexia is a mistaken medical diagnosis.[3] We are not doctors, and none of us have actually examined Weil. The point is rather that whether or not Simone Weil suffered from a medical condition involving an eating disorder, it is asking too much to have us believe that this by itself can account for her life-long preoccupation with food. The word 'medical', here, gives the illusion of understanding. It suggests precisely that reductive attitude to science – not to say, the 'science of the mind [or soul?]' – of which Weil herself was rightly sceptical. Science in this sense is not so much an alternative to religion as an alternative religion, and 'so far as the prestige of science is concerned', wrote Weil, 'there are no such people nowadays as unbelievers'.[4] It is all too familiar – a simple solution to a complex problem. Explanation by stereotype: the anorexic young girl, the self-hating Jew, the incomplete virgin.

There was, however, nothing simple about Weil's death, as there is not about the phenomenon of eating. It is not simply a question of health and medicine. Metaphysically speaking, as Weil was well aware, eating is a form of violence – of destruction and assimilation. In eating, we do to our food what Caesar and the Roman Empire did to Gaul. This is brought out forcefully by Leon Kass in his illuminating study, *The Hungry Soul: Eating and the Perfecting of Our Nature*.[5] Eating, in particular digestion, constitutes a singular relationship to reality. On the surface, it may seem to represent the most primitive, the most basic form of cognition, as when a child or an animal tries to get to know something new by putting it into its mouth, to taste, chew and finally digest it. In fact, however, regarded through an ontological lens, digestion does not assimilate the knower to the known, but rather, just the reverse. Whereas, as Kass puts it, echoing Aristotle's *De Anima*, 'in thinking, the thinking mind seems to become one with the thing thought', in eating, 'we do not become the thing we eat; rather, the edible becomes assimilated to what we are.'[6]

In perception, says Aristotle, the mind takes in the *form* of the perceived object without the *matter*, whereas, as Kass puts it, 'the edible object is thoroughly transformed by and re-formed by the eater.'[7] When I eat a hamburger, I do not become a burger; rather it becomes (a part of) me. Digestion 'depends on physical contact with and destruction of its object; what is tasted is never a being but only some of its chemical materials'.[8] For 'taste, in contrast with sight, can reveal almost nothing about the nature or way of life of what is eaten'.[9] More precisely, in eating, we destroy the consumed object by separating its form from its matter –the very definition of death, according to Plato in the *Phaedo* – incorporating what was its matter into our own substance.

Our life, then, depends on our bringing about another's death. 'The great paradox of eating', says Kass, '[is that] to preserve life and form, living form necessarily destroys life and form',[10] which means that man, as omnivorous, is in essence 'morally ambiguous'. Man, the knowing animal, is at the same time the universal eater whose very life turns on the destruction of other living beings. 'Omnivorousness', says Kass, 'means, in principle, the willingness to homogenize and destroy the world as formed . . . to swallow and turn it into oneself.'[11] Man, the omnivorous being, the morally ambiguous animal, stands thus in radical need of guidance, of salvation, if he is not to lose himself in the course of the very enterprise of preserving his existence. In Kass's study the focus is on the guidance provided by the strictures on eating given in the Hebrew Bible that are intended to transform us from animals that *feed* into human beings that *eat*. What is more relevant to an understanding of Weil, however, is the special place reserved for eating in the Christian Gospels and the Catholic liturgy. Before we approach the significance in Weil's thought, however, of the Last Supper and the Catholic ceremony of communion, we need to understand how powerfully the metaphysics of eating affected her.

'The great trouble in human life', wrote Weil, as we saw earlier, 'is that gazing and eating are two different operations.'[12] The highest human activity, which is for Weil 'almost a miracle', openness to being – what she calls 'attending' to the being of others, to their suffering – granted us not by the mouth but by the eye, or rather, the mind's eye, is in itself insufficient to support our existence. We cannot live by looking but only by eating – that is, by destroying. Indeed, what passes for love among human beings, which should be a form of beholding or appreciation, resembles more closely eating or digestion. We eat our friends and lovers. 'In our love', says Weil, 'we are cannibals'[13] – assimilating others to us, rather than us to them. '[The corpses in the *Iliad*]', she writes, 'are far dearer to the vultures than to their wives. Such is human love. One loves only what one can eat.'[14] That which we love most, what is most lovable, the beautiful, as Plato insists in the *Symposium*, we destroy by eating. Indeed, as noted earlier, 'depravity', according to Weil, 'and crime are . . . perhaps always, in their essence, attempts to eat beauty, to eat what we should only look at.'[15] Is there any wonder that food and sex were for Weil, throughout her life – a life informed by taking seriously those insights of Plato's that others appreciate at most as mental exercises – not so much sources of consolation as spiritual tests that God or nature has placed before us?

She was unable, of course, though not through lack of trying, to do entirely without the consolation of food. She had more success with sex. The 'Red Virgin' really was one. Though she was not in the least bit prudish and had acquired from her friend, Colette Peignot, a more than passing acquaintance with the dark side of sex, for herself romance would forever be a stranger.[16] She took her readings of Plato and the Gospels to the limit. 'Instead of seeing love of God as a sublimated form of carnal desire', she wrote, 'as many people [i.e. Freud] in our wretched epoch do, Plato thinks that carnal desire is a corruption, a degradation, of love of God.'[17] Plato did perhaps think this, but he had his own problems,[18] and, if taken as a recommendation to engage in an ascetic life, this is probably one of those passages that should be taken with a healthy grain of salt. Weil, however, skipped the salt entirely. As her friend Thibon knew only too well, her self-image, down here, in the world of 'gravity', was swallowed up by a black hole of self-denial.[19]

And there is indeed no sunlight that can enliven her picture of Adam and Eve, who, she said, 'sought for divinity in vital energy – a tree, fruit. But it is [in fact] prepared for us on dead wood, geometrically squared, where a corpse is hanging.'[20] When she thinks of the stirrings of desire, Simone Weil comes up not with an apple, but a corpse.

This is not to deny that her thought here is profound, but only to comment on the morbidity of her image. The desire to know good and evil, to become like God, she is saying, cannot, like our vital desires – for food, for sex – be satisfied by consuming the right food, fruit from some divine tree. Yet what, then, of the Eucharist? This, too, for Weil, is misused if seen as merely a replacement of Eve's apple. Just this, she believed, was missed by Henri Bergson, for whom 'religious faith appears after the manner of a "pink" pill . . . which confers an astonishing amount of vitality . . . (*élan vital*).'[21] At the same time, she insisted that if undertaken 'in the right spirit', so to speak, sexual activity itself can represent the love of God. 'To reproach mystics', she writes in her notebooks, 'with loving God by means of the faculty of sexual love is as though one were to reproach a painter with making pictures by means of colours composed of material substances. We haven't anything else with which to love.'[22]

And yet was this something with which Weil herself could love? God, she said, does not provide a supernatural cure but rather a supernatural use for affliction. She was clearly afflicted with a self-image that made sexual love impossible. Her deep admiration for the virtue of chastity should not be confused with what appears to have been an emotional incapacity for receiving love. Something inside her was broken. She could not fix it, but only transform her sadness into a kind of food for divine thought. But the sadness remained. At Normale, one summer day, 'when she was picking plums in the country', writes Cabaud, 'she climbed a wall and couldn't get down again. A young man stretched out his hands to her. At the implications behind this gesture, either from modesty or because she felt bound to refuse assistance, she trembled all over.'[23] As Cabaud notes, 'there seems to have been an intensity of affective life which no one understood.' At the mere thought of being touched by a man, she trembled. And it was not only men. Sylvie Weil recounts a story of when her aunt and her mother, Eveline (André's wife), were alone together in André's apartment in Paris, spending the night telling each other stories over a jar of brandied cherries.[24] Eveline, outgoing and affectionate, reached over to touch Simone's hair. She recoiled as if bitten by a snake.

Saddest of all, perhaps, is an episode that occurred when she was teaching at Bourges. She was entertaining her new friends, a young couple, the Coulombs. ('Simone always had a soft spot for couples', writes Cabaud.[25]) She told them about her visit to Spain, mentioning that 'a Spanish coal-trimmer had once kissed her in Barcelona . . . Coulomb jokingly asked if the man was drunk. Simone burst into tears.'[26] It does not take away from the insights revealed in her Christological reflections on Plato and the story of Eve to note that she craved the warmth and intimacy of a love she believed, to the depths of her soul, no one could feel for her. That she was herself beautiful added insult to injury. What made it still worse was her devotion to the beautiful, as such, which for her was anything but an abstraction. 'Absolute beauty', she wrote, 'is something as concrete as sensible objects'.[27]

As was the case with Plato, it was for her a bridge to God. '[T]he Beautiful', she said, 'is the image of the Good.'[28] We all desire the beautiful, of course, but 'the beautiful is that which we desire without wishing to eat it. We desire that it should be.'[29] And yet human life is characterized by a constant state of privation, of needs that, on an ontological level, we can never really fulfil, since the fundamental human desires for food and sex are, as Plato insisted, in their strictly human form, but images of our true desire for what is truly real, and at the same time beyond our grasp, beyond our ability – as embodied creatures, beings in the material realm, the realm of gravity, not grace – to consume and digest. Yet 'in the event of privation', says Weil, 'one cannot help turning to anything whatever that is edible. There is only one remedy for that: a chlorophyll conferring the faculty of feeding on light.'[30] A supernatural chlorophyll conferring the faculty of feeding on light: that is Simone Weil's conception of the divine. How, then, can beings like us be granted such a transfiguration?

The answer for Weil to the question of how gazing can be transformed into nourishment, into eating, comes from the Word given in the Gospels and, according to her, prefigured in Plato's philosophy – the *Logos* that is embodied, for Christians, not just in the teachings but in the very life of Christ. And yet the suggestion is made, as we have seen, that perhaps she was 'attracted to Christianity because of its obsessive emphasis on food'.[31] The emphasis on Christianity gives the false impression that the question of eating is less central to the religion of Weil's ancestors, the religion most commentators cannot bring themselves to forgive Weil for 'abandoning'. Yet who can deny the deep significance of the Jewish dietary laws, the true meaning of which Kass, in the study on which we have been drawing, has done much to illuminate? Who can deny the significance of the breaking of bread in the ceremony of the Passover? If Weil chose Christianity over Judaism, it was not the mere consequence of her anorexia driving her to adopt the religion where food played the most prominent role. Indeed, the two religions pivot around a common vertex, the Passover seder. For the Christian ceremony of the Eucharist, the taking of holy communion, so close to Weil's heart and so central to the Catholic religion Weil loved yet could not bring herself to join, is of course derived from the Last Supper of Christ, a Passover seder shared with his disciples.

In his reinterpretation of this traditional Jewish ceremony, Jesus bade his disciples eat the bread he was breaking, which would be his body, and drink the wine, his blood. Du Plessix Gray speaks of the 'cannibalistic associations of Holy Communion',[32] but what emerges clearly from Kass's study is that cannibalism has in fact exactly the opposite meaning from that of the communion. The cannibal, Kass points out, 'treat[s] as respectable and worthy only what is merely *familiar* and *one's own* [i.e. one's tribe]. Cannibalism is perhaps the radical embodiment of such a mistake.'[33] For the cannibal, the other means the other tribe, which is seen, in Kass's words, as potential 'meat, not mate' – i.e. as food. In communion, however, it is not that the host is considered consumable because it is 'outside', and therefore 'below', the dignity of the tribe. On the contrary, what is eaten is not man but God – someone not beneath but rather far above the level of the tribe.

When God is 'eaten', he is not digested; what was God does not become man, but rather the reverse. The eater becomes the eaten. When one consumes the communion wafer, God does not conform to us, but rather we to him. Man is assimilated to the form of the divine, not the divine to man. The Eucharist is not nourishment for the body, but rather food for the soul. It is not, says the distinguished British philosopher Elizabeth Anscombe in 'On Transubstantiation', 'like digestion, in which what you eat turns into you'.[34] In a sense, then, the communion is a ceremony of what might be called 'reverse eating' – the only way in this world, the world of gravity, in which eating can be transformed into gazing. And our recognition of this possibility is not granted to us by our intelligence, by the faculty that guides us through the world of facts. 'The Eucharist', says Weil, 'should not . . . be an object of belief for the part of me which apprehends facts . . . Only with that part of us which is made for the supernatural should we adhere to these mysteries.'[35]

That, surely – not her supposed anorexia, her hatred of her Jewish body, her blindness to the 'Jewish beauty of her mind' – is the source of Weil's love for the ceremony of communion of the Catholic faith. In the miracle of communion, for Weil, we nourish ourselves not by eating, but by being eaten – by becoming food for God. And like Plato before her, it is beauty – the beauty of God, the beauty of God-being-in-the-world – that draws us in. 'The beauty of the world', she writes, 'is the mouth of a labyrinth. The unwary individual who on entering takes a few steps is soon unable to find the opening . . . [but] if he goes on walking, it is absolutely certain that he will finally arrive at the center . . . And there, God is waiting to eat him.'[36]

Whereas for many, if not most believers, religion serves as a source of consolation, for Weil, this is a perversion of the idea of God. For her, as for Plato, we must seek the being most worthy of being loved, the divine, not desire, as children do, to be loved. 'Love', she writes, 'is not consolation; it is light.'[37] Whereas eating is a source of nourishment and consolation, a respite from our mortal hunger, 'reverse eating', the taking of the Eucharist, concerns our immortal part. 'The eternal part of the soul', writes Weil, 'feeds on hunger . . . [It] consumes the mortal part of the soul and transforms it. The hunger of our soul is hard to bear, but there is no other remedy for our disease.'[38]

Is this really to be characterized as mere 'spiritual anorexia'? On the contrary, is not Weil correct that 'when God has become as full of significance as the treasure is for the miser, we have to tell ourselves insistently that he does not exist'?[39] Reverse eating, then, the consuming of the Eucharist, is not merely, as it were, 'eating with the sign reversed', supplying not physical but spiritual consolation. It is not a natural but rather a supernatural chlorophyll towards which Weil is directing us.[40]

Did she find it? Why, if it was the ontology of eating that concerned Weil, the transformation of our immortal self through the consumption not *of* but *by* the divine, did Weil spend a lifetime, in effect, starving her mortal coil, her merely human body? Why, when she contracted tuberculosis, did she refuse the nourishment necessary to help her survive? If this is a psychological question, then we must leave it to the doctors. It is no part of the present study to deny that Weil's life, like that of all human beings, had a complex psychological dimension, a dimension that includes elements of a disturbed self-image, a tortured relationship to her Jewish heritage, a love affair/rejection of her French homeland. What we have been disputing is that we can *reduce* the philosophy and theology of Simone Weil to her autobiography, to her psychology. Whatever role psychological factors may have played, then, in Weil's life-long preoccupation with eating, her diet that was never far from being a form of starvation, we cannot, if we are to do justice to Weil, ignore or belittle the deep role played not only by her philosophy but by her embodiment of her philosophy. For the charge of *imitatio dei, imitatio Christi* does, after all, apply to Weil.

Already as a young child, as we have seen, Weil expressed her solidarity with soldiers on the front lines who had to do without by herself going without food – sugar at first, and then substantive meals as she grew older. Early and late, she evinced a Christ-like quality of giving physical expression to her sympathy with the plight of others – and what is more real, for the physical body, than the deprivation of nourishment, the sine qua non for its very survival? And nothing was more real for Weil than the suffering of others – a capacity for not just sympathy but empathy that had amazed Simone de Beauvoir at the École Normale. For many, this capacity represents a kind of illness, but it is no more a sign of disease than was the life of Christ. The reaction of Weil to the sufferings of others – in particular, of others outside her 'tribe', with whom she had no visible connection – was not so much emotional as ontological. It was a question of *being*, more than *feeling*. Not just the thought but the very life of Simone Weil represents a kind of photographic plate in which the invisible wounds of others, in particular, those whose share of being is the most tenuous – the sick, the outcast, the abandoned, the suffering – become manifest. The final march of Koch's bacilli into the lungs of Simone Weil was only the last and most visible sign of the suffering she had taken on herself throughout her 34 years of life.

In gradually withdrawing nourishment from her body, always in sympathy and solidarity with the poor, Weil was using up her physical self in order to fulfil her life's work – making her body the fuel and substance of a spiritual fire.[41] As Chris Kraus writes in *Aliens and Anorexia*, '[Weil] was a performative philosopher. Her body was [her] material.'[42] As Weil herself wrote, 'the body is a lever for salvation. But in what way? *What is the right way to use it?*'[43] By causing her body to eat itself, she was in effect feeding herself to God – as in the ceremony of the communion. She was living on light. But you can't live on light. As she wrote in her Notebooks, 'sanctity is a transmutation like the Eucharist'.[44] The lowliest peasant, she believed, if he labours in the right spirit, becomes sanctified, food for Christ. 'If I grow thin from labour in the fields, my flesh really becomes wheat. If that wheat is used for the host, it becomes Christ's flesh. Anyone who labours with this intention should become a saint.'[45]

Yet, as Chris Kraus points out, there seems always to be an attempt to 'treat [Weil's] philosophical writings as a kind of biographical key. Impossible to conceive a female life that might extend outside itself. Impossible to accept the self-destruction of a woman as *strategic*.'[46] Weil as the 'anorexic philosopher'? 'Though Friedrich Nietzsche', writes Kraus, 'suffered from blinding headaches, *The Gay Science* is not interpreted as a Philosophy of Headaches.'[47] Weil's death, in effect, from starvation, *means something*. What, we must ask, is that meaning?

One answer that must be rejected is that we should all become ascetics. One does not honour Weil's teachings by going on a strict diet. As with all great teachers, it is all too easy to mistake the word for the spirit. And the end is always the same: idolatry. No memory can be made safe from perversion. Sylvie Weil[48] tells a story of being invited when twelve or thirteen to snacks at a classmate's home, where she was discovered to be related to her famous aunt. 'Your aunt killed herself from starvation, right?', said her friend's grandmother. 'She was a saint', said the mother, 'according to our priest . . . a veritable ascetic . . . (or was it a mystic?) . . .'. Sylvie, 'busy eating a cookie, and trying not to leave crumbs', does not know how to respond. After all, she protests, 'I was normal, I ate a tarte, also part of a flan . . . even though the blood of practically a saint ran in my veins.' Yet, 'I felt guilty of a betrayal, without knowing precisely whom I betrayed.'

The real betrayal, however, would be to make a fetish out of Simone's hunger. Hers was no more a philosophy of eating than it was a philosophy of headaches. The Eucharist is not a component of a 'religious diet', and Simone Weil was not writing a cookbook for healthy souls. If there is no apple we can eat to save ourselves, there is equally none with which we can save ourselves by not eating. 'I do not read', said Weil, 'I eat.'[49] We in turn, must not simply read such lines. We must eat.

8

On the Jewish Question

Saints are not given to us for the sake of comfort.

Gustave Thibon

Simone Weil hastened her death from tuberculosis through self-starvation, but as we have seen, there is no force to the claim that she 'might have speeded her death through her loathing for her Jewish body'. Was Simone Weil, however, a Jew?[1] To the orthodox, the answer is simple: since she had a Jewish mother, the matter is settled. But how did Simone view herself, especially in light of the harshness of her critique of her ancestral religion? For years, the story went around, encouraged by Simone and André, that it was only in their teens that they had learned of their Jewish heritage. 'I even remember that during the [Great] War', André said in an interview with Malcolm Muggeridge,[2] 'someone told me I was Jewish and I just didn't know what they meant.' That this was all a myth, however, should have been obvious. 'André and Simone had carefully supported the little familial novel', writes Sylvie Weil,[3] 'which consisted of making themselves believe, then making others believe, that as kids they didn't know they were Jewish . . . [However] André was called Abraham, he was circumcised . . . his grandmother Eugenie read her prayer book (in Hebrew, evidently) . . . [His mother] Selma scattered her correspondence with Yiddish words'. Are we to believe that the 'two-headed genius', André and Simone, was on this one point prey to an unaccustomed stupidity?

With the question posed to her father so bluntly, writes Sylvie, 'André smiled'.

To André, it appears, the whole question of ancestry was a diversion. To Simone, however, things stood otherwise. 'I am paralyzed', she once wrote to her friend Boris Souvarine, 'by the sentiment that I am accused of descending from a people who couldn't find anything better to give to humanity than Jehovah.'[4] Unlike Wittgenstein, however, also conflicted over his Jewish heritage, she never attempted to hide it. Her friends were spared the ordeal Wittgenstein's were forced to endure when, in typical fashion, once he had a change of heart, he chose to engage them in a series of 'confessions' dedicated to revealing his Jewish roots.[5] Simone's friend and biographer Simone Pétrement records that once when they were in their late teens 'some students in the Latin Quarter were shouting the name of the newspaper they were selling and added, "Anti-foreigner and anti-Yid." I hadn't heard them clearly and asked her what they had said. She . . . explained: "It's a name they give the Jews," and then blushed.'[6] (Equally moving is Pétrement's comment: 'I hope that that was the only time I hurt her by such thoughtless behavior.')

What Simone also made no attempt to hide was her dislike, her harsh disdain for much of the Hebrew Bible and many of the traditions, ancient as well as modern, of her ancestors. 'About 1934, she said one day to [a family friend] Bercher', writes Pétrement, 'as a joke, "personally, I am an anti-Semite." . . . [Later] she agreed [with Bercher] that she was not really an anti-Semite and that the Jews she disliked were those who regarded themselves as Jews before all else, and so *separated* themselves from other men.'[7]

Not all, however, agree with Pétrement that Simone's innocent interpretation of her unguarded comment is the correct one, especially in light of the vituperation she poured, in a number of contexts, on ancient as well as not so ancient Israel. When *Gravity and Grace* first appeared, many otherwise sympathetic readers in the Jewish community were shocked, not to say, horrified. It was the last chapter, 'Israel', that offended – the only chapter, curiously, missing in the original English translation of the book. To be sure, the book itself was never intended for publication. Indeed, it is not a book Simone Weil actually wrote. It consists of passages from her notebooks that her friend, Gustave Thibon, with her permission, selected and assembled for publication. These facts, however, do little to diminish the force of the final chapter. Nor do the previous sections of the book, which prepare the way, soften the impact. True, Weil makes clear early in the book that 'God is given to us as powerful or perfect: it is for us to choose', and that for her, the Jehovah of the Hebrew Bible was powerful before being perfect. True, she viewed the idea of the 'Chosen People' and the 'promised land' as examples of idolatry, worse, by far, than the idolatry of other gods or even 'totems' condemned by the ancient Israelites. None of these observations keep one from gasping when one reads in the final chapter that, 'Christianity has become totalitarian, conquering, exterminating . . . It attached itself to Jehovah as it did to Christ.' And it gets worse: 'The curse of Israel weighs upon Christianity. Atrocities, the Inquisition, extermination of heretics . . . that was Israel. Capitalism, that was Israel'.[8]

It is understandable, therefore, that in his much quoted 'Sainte Simone',[9] the distinguished novelist and literary critic George Steiner chastises those who are inclined to sanctify Weil for failing to acknowledge what he calls 'the central issue of Simone Weil's Judaism and rejection of Judaism'. To ignore the issue of Weil's attitude to Judaism together with the storm of protest it has engendered is simply to fail to appreciate the significance of Simone Weil in today's world. Steiner is correct to point out that 'this issue is (as, perhaps in the case of Wittgenstein) not only immensely complicated . . . it is, at many points, highly unpleasant, indeed repellent.' What is less obvious, however, is whether it is not tendentious for him to say that 'when her own people were being harried to bestial extinction, [she] refused baptism into the Catholic Church because "Roman Catholicism was too Jewish"',[10] without at the same time drawing attention to what her friend Thibon has said,[11] that she did not want to give the impression, by accepting baptism, that she was *separating* herself from other Jews, or indeed, from non-Catholics. In this, Steiner is hardly alone. When one speaks of Simone Weil and the Jewish question, the enormity of the response to her writings is every bit as significant as the writings themselves.

Alfred Kazin, thus, in 'A Genius of the Spiritual Life', writes that 'she was Jewish, and looked it[!] . . . [but] despised herself for being a Jew . . . Assimilation never saw a Jew more eager to despise herself.'[12] Similarly, Rachel Brenner in *Writing as Resistance: Four Women Against the Holocaust*,[13] writes that Weil 'denied her Jewish identity' and 'desired to obliterate her Jewishness' due to her 'inability to accept herself as a Jew' and to her search for 'deliverance from the burden of Jewishness', while W. Rabi famously wrote in '*La Conception weilienne de la Création Rencontre avec la Kabbale juive*' of 'those who *abandon* us [Jews], like Simone Weil, or who *slander* us, like her'.[14] Jeffrey Mehlman, meanwhile, as we saw earlier, writes in *Emigré New York* that, 'she was a Jew who, in that conflict [the war against Hitler] had at the outset switched sides.'[15] Indeed, according to Mehlman, 'the figure most deeply committed to risking her life in the struggle against Hitler did so out of a sense of things so profoundly anti-Semitic as to the set the mind reeling.'[16]

The resentment that has attended Weil's rejection of Judaism has, moreover, been exacerbated by the widespread conception that in spite of, or even because of, the fact that she refused to be identified as a Jew, she demonstrated that she was somehow 'essentially Jewish'. It is a painful irony that Weil's extreme disaffection with what she saw as, in effect, the 'racial lens' by which so much in Judaism is viewed – the same lens adopted by anti-Semites – has been applied to this very disaffection, which has itself been taken as evidence that she was, after all, a Jew, indeed, 'in the highest degree'. Thus even her champion T. S. Eliot has written that 'Simone Weil was three things in the highest degree: French, Jewish, and Christian.'[17] Eliot, clearly, is not referring simply to Weil's racial ancestry, since it would be nonsense to say that her ancestry was Jewish 'in the highest degree'. To what else, then, can he be appealing, if not to a classical racial stereotype?

Sadly, even her spiritual companion, the remarkable Gustave Thibon, could not help commenting that 'no doubt she owed this hardness of green fruit . . . to her racial origin . . . [while] her passionate anti-semitism is the most striking evidence of her descent.'[18] Indeed, asks Thibon, 'is there anything *more Jewish*[!] than . . . the urge to examine and test the great realities . . . ?' And yet Thibon's observation is more the rule than the exception, as witnessed by George Steiner's remark in 'Sainte Simone' that '*in a radically Jewish sense*[!], she loved language supremely'.[19] A strange remark, given that Simone Weil, was, after all, a *French* writer who used to recite Racine and Corneille by heart as a young child. For Steiner, it appears, and many others, all that is relevant to her love of language – the great French language – is that Simone's grand-parents attended synagogue. No doubt, if Weil had been a gourmet instead of an ascetic, they would have attributed her love of food not to her having spent her childhood in the legendary eateries of Paris, but to her 'radically Jewish' love of gefilte fish.

Thus has a person who set her face against all racializing, *whether on behalf of or against Jews* or any other group, been subject to the crudest of racial stereotyping. As night follows day, of course, it has been concluded that the heritage Weil rejected represented 'her own people'. Yet, as Thibon has written, despite her heritage, she simply did not identify with the Jewish community. In the (in)famous letter we encountered earlier which she wrote in 1940 to the Minister of Education of the Vichy government upon being dismissed from her teaching position in accordance with the new racial laws,[20] she asks: 'Does this word ['Jew'] designate a religion? I have never been in a synagogue, and have never witnessed a Jewish religious ceremony.' Does it designate a race? 'In that case, I have no reason to believe that I have any link to the people who inhabited Palestine two thousand years ago.' 'If there is a religious tradition', she concluded, 'which I regard as my patrimony, it is the Catholic tradition. In short, mine is the Christian, French, Greek, tradition.' However one reacts to this letter, could Weil have made it any clearer that she did *not* view Jews as 'her people'? She was not raised in, was not familiar with, was not attracted to the Jewish religion or culture, did not believe in the very concept of race – in fact, considered it the bane of western civilization – did not identify with or empathize with her Jewish ancestors. To quote Fania Pascal, after Wittgenstein 'confessed' to her his Jewish-ness: 'some Jew!'[21]

Yet according to the Jewish religion and tradition, of course, she was nevertheless Jewish, since she had a Jewish mother – though, as she pointed out in her letter to the Vichy Minister, strictly, this just pushes the problem of identification back one generation, since what made her mother Jewish was that she, in turn, had a Jewish mother, and so on . . . Of course, every religion, needless to say, is free to determine its own criteria of membership, but it is surely deeply misleading to characterize someone as 'abandoning' a membership they themselves never recognized in the first place. A choice must be made. Who is the final arbiter of whether or not one belongs to a religion or a people – a distinction, to be sure, that is blurred in Judaism. For Weil, it is the individual who determines his own spiritual identity, the direction of his soul. Nor was this a belief confined to her religious views. As we saw earlier, in her response to the collectivism of her erstwhile Marxist colleagues, she wrote in her essay on the 'Proletarian Revolution' that 'we wish to uphold not the collectivity but the individual as the supreme value'.[22]

Is it not, after all, perverse that intellectuals who chose to identify themselves as Jews *simply because Hitler viewed them thus* have
received high praise and are held up as paradigms by which to
measure Weil's failings – though they are, after all, examples of
souls who abandoned their birthright and granted Hitler, of all
people, the privilege of establishing their Jewish identity? Yet Sylvie
Courtine-Denamy writes in *Three Women in Dark Times: Edith Stein,
Hanna Arendt, Simone Weil*,[23] that '[Hanna Arendt] attached no
importance to the fact [that she was Jewish] until Hitler's perse -
cutions endangered German Jewry. At that point she became truly
Jewish, adopting a motto of Pindar's that Nietzsche cites: "Become
what you are".'[24] Was not Arendt's motto, rather, 'Become what
Hitler says you are?' Is Weil really to be condemned for refusing to
adopt such a motto? Is she to be criticized, in turn, for resisting the
efforts of the Jewish community, despite her protests to the contrary,
to tell her who she 'really' is – to condemn her for refusing to wear
the label, the yellow star, they have pinned on her? Is what Weil said
to Thibon – that in certain respects Nazis and Jews, the murderers
and their victims, 'hunted on the same ground'[25] – to be dismissed
as mere prejudice, as it so often is, as mere anti-Semitism?[26]

The philosopher Karl Popper, too, let us recall, refused to let
either the Nazis or the Jewish community dictate his identity. And
for this courageous stance he, too, as we have seen, has been cast
as a self-hating Jew, a closet anti-Semite.[27] And the examples of
Weil and Popper are far from unique. There exists a kind of cottage
industry that attempts to enlist into the Jewish community the most
famous apostate of all, Baruch/Benedict Spinoza, though, as in the
case of Weil, it is hard to see how a human being could possibly
have been clearer that he declined membership in that community
– the community that itself, during his lifetime, literally kicked him
out – i.e. excommunicated him. The comedy (or tragedy?) of trying
to enlist Spinoza against his will as a true son of the community
that he himself rejected before it formally rejected him is recorded

in detail by Allan Nadler in 'Romancing Spinoza'.[28] Like Weil, Spinoza (whom Weil adored) 'clearly favored Christianity over Judaism'. Like Weil, he 'repeatedly and effusively praised the message of Jesus'. Like Weil, he rejected baptism – though unlike her, he was never tempted. In neither case, however, was there a lingering allegiance to the Jewish community that was their heritage. Yet, as Adler notes, 'in the 20th century, and extending into our own day, many liberal Jewish scholars and intellectuals have . . . [i]nsisted on his *essential "Jewishness"*.'

To put a stop, in turn, to the 'romancing of Simone Weil', one need only recall a conversation Thibon had with Simone that echoes her letter to the Minister of Education. 'Simone Weil said to me', he writes, '"what is it to be Jewish? Is it a race? Listen, it must be mixed. I do not feel one way more than another. Thus, in every case I am not a racist [or 'racialist'?]. Is it a religion? Well then, this religion is not mine at all . . ." Thus . . . one cannot say that she had *betrayed a community*. She did not think that she *belonged* to that community. From that community she felt herself uprooted'.[29]

The question before us, then, is not why Simone Weil rejected 'her own people', but rather why she was so critical of the religion, and the history, of the Jewish people. There has been a widespread myth that as a child, she was beleaguered by her Jewish heritage. 'Though her ancestors had been Jewish', writes Leslie Fiedler, 'the faith had quite disappeared in her immediate family', though among remote relatives, 'it had become something cold, oppressive and meaninglessly legalistic to a degree that made Simone Weil all of her life incapable of judging fairly the merits of Judaism.'[30] Almost everything Fiedler states here is false. In the chapter 'Stuffed Carp', of her memoir about her father and aunt, Sylvie Weil sketches a touching picture of her maternal grandmother, Eugenie Weill [sic], who never stopped inviting the Weil family to her yearly seder, and who, from time to time, moved in with the Weils with her 'kosher casserole and plates as well as her book of Hebrew prayers'. 'Would Simone have been traumatized', asks Sylvie, 'because her grandmother wouldn't have taken her purse nor her umbrella when she walked on Saturdays? Because she didn't eat pork? or shrimp?'[31] A stranger in France with a weak command of the language, Eugenie was, says Sylvie, 'a very sweet grandmother who demanded only that she could adore the little one that she called Simonele.'

This is what is supposed to have turned Simone against the religion of her ancestors? And what about her mother's family, the Reinherzs? They attended synagogue at Antwerp and observed the holidays. Her grandfather Adolphe wrote a book of Hebrew poems. Bound in red Moroccan leather, it disappeared in the course of time, to the dismay of André. This is the 'oppressive' family background that is supposed to have prevented Simone from being able to make a fair assessment of the Jewish faith?

Fiedler, however, is far from alone. Many have tried to find 'explanations' of Weil's attitude to Jewry – her supposed close encounters as a child with harsh religious practices, her inability to bear the burden of her Jewishness, her typically Jewish self-hatred, her crystallization of over 150 years of the spiritlessness of French Jewry, bent on self-annihilation, etc. – and when none have proved convincing, declared Weil's attitude a mystery. Even as deep a thinker as Marie Cabaud Meaney, author of what is surely one of the most penetrating books ever written on Weil, writes that 'one may wonder *why* the Jewish religion is such a blind spot in Weil, for she never gave it much sympathy or attention.'[32]

The well-known words, however, from Simone's teacher at the Lycée, Alain, about the Hebrew Bible provide the first clue. Alain, as we have seen, was outraged by 'this God of the [Hebrew] Bible who is always massacring'.[33] It is possible Weil was influenced here by Alain, but, to recall what Isaac Newton said in another context, *hypotheses non fingo*, it is not necessary to invent hypotheses. One simply has to *read* the Hebrew Bible with open eyes and without prejudice to realize why the primary complaint Weil has is that it is difficult to see how the (to her eyes) warlike, vengeful God of the Hebrew Bible, Yahweh, can be identified as the 'father' of Jesus – the man who gave the Sermon on the Mount.

Let us remind ourselves of just a few of the massacres in the Hebrew Bible[34] – passages that are all too often simply 'passed over in silence', to adapt a phrase from Wittgenstein. Everyone is familiar with the Passover story from Exodus, in which the Jewish people were finally freed from their years in slavery in Egypt. But how exactly were they set free? On the appointed day, each man in the community of Israel was to slaughter a lamb and smear its blood on his door-frame. 'On that same night', said the Lord to Moses and Aaron, 'I will pass through Egypt and strike down every firstborn – both men and animals . . . When I see the blood [on your door-frames], I will pass over you.'[35] And it came to pass. 'At midnight, the Lord struck down all the firstborn in Egypt, from the firstborn of Pharaoh . . . to the firstborn of the prisoner, who was in the dungeon, and the firstborn of all the livestock as well . . . [T]here was wailing in Egypt, for there was not a house without someone dead.' Is it merely her 'Jewish self-hatred', her supposed 'anti-Semitism', that leads Weil to question whether Jesus (or the Father he invokes) could have descended from the Sermon on the Mount to carry out this massacre?

Though led from slavery by the Lord, the Jewish people have relapses. Everyone knows the story, further into Exodus, of their worship of the Golden Calf. A rebuke is inevitable: 'This is what the Lord, the God of Israel, says: "Each man strap a sword to his side. Go back and forth through the camp from one end to the other, each killing his brother and friend and neighbor." . . . [A]nd that day about three thousand of the people died. Then Moses said: "You have been set apart to the Lord today, for you were against your own sons and brothers, and he has blessed you this day."' As Elaine Scarry notes, 'passages throughout the Old Testament that deal with . . . graven images . . . remind the offenders that God is a disembodied voice . . . hovering on the other side of a weapon.'[36] Could Jesus, who rebuked his disciple for striking at the ear of a Roman soldier coming to take him away, have given these instructions? Is it prejudice against 'her own people' that leads Weil to ask this question?

Finally, later still, Joshua sees what appears to be a man with his sword drawn who tells him that he is 'commander of the army of the Lord'. And the Lord said to Joshua, 'I have delivered Jericho into your hands.' And Joshua said to his people: 'Only Rahab the prostitute and all who are with her will be spared, because she hid the spies we sent.' Then the trumpets sounded, the wall came down, and 'they devoted the city to the Lord and destroyed with sword every living thing in it – men and women, young and old, cattle, sheep and donkeys.' Is it simply Weil's 'Jewish self-loathing' that leads her to suggest that the idea behind the Christian Crusades, the 'armies of Christ', harks back to the Jewish idea of the 'army of the Lord', not to the Christ who spoke of turning the other cheek? Is there some confusion in her questioning whether the same spirit that animates Christ's sermons could have inspired the destruction with the sword of every living thing in Jericho? 'To believe God can order men to commit atrocious acts of injustice and cruelty', said Weil, 'is the greatest mistake it is possible to make with regard to him.'[37] Do Weil's critics wish to deny this proposition? Does agreeing with her make one an anti-Semite?[38]

Of course there is more to the Hebrew Bible than these stories, but at the same time, there is not less. These passages exist, they must be accounted for. True, the massacres they represent are ancient ones, but, as Weil said, 'does time make it some different type of business?'[39] In thousands of years, the massacres carried out by the Nazis will also be ancient history. Will that, as Weil says, 'make them a different kind of business'? Her friend Maurice Schumann spoke with her in 1942. 'She told me', he says, 'she had, during the last months of her time in France, vainly searched for a Catholic priest who disavowed the God of Saul.'[40] Seeing Schumann's reaction, she asked him, 'Have you read the book of Saul?' He responded that he hadn't. 'Do you know', she told him, 'that if Saul is punished by the Eternal, it's not because he killed all the Amalecites, including the children and women [who] passed over the tip of his dagger, but because he killed all except one; he pardoned the king.' And then comes a question that stops one cold: 'How do we condemn a holocaust if we have not condemned all past holocausts?' Do those who have heaped scorn on Weil for her 'anti-Semitic' reading of the Bible have a reply to this?

'Now I remember', adds Schumann, 'that in 1942 we did not know yet the existence of the extermination camps.' He recalls how just before he left London, in 1944, he saw on a wall a political cartoon depicting 'how it begins', with two women making a slur against Jews, and then 'how it ends', with a depiction of a Nazi shoving a woman and her child towards a crematorium. 'My thoughts immediately went back to Simone Weil', he says, 'who had died a few months previously, and I said to myself, 'What marvelous and atrocious prescience! She used the word "holocaust" when at that time no one had used it yet, and more, the word, "genocide"; but she had seen, in certain verses of the Old Testament that she could not accept, a justification for genocide of which she felt, if she adhered to it, if she accepted it, if she did not repudiate it, this acceptance of genocide caused her necessarily to no longer have the right to condemn the Hitlerian genocide.' Do those who have been quick to throw stones at Weil really wish to associate themselves with the other side of this argument? Should Mehlman consider retracting his statement that 'she was a Jew who, in that conflict [the war against Hitler] had at the outset switched sides'? Would he still want to assert that '[she took part] in the struggle against Hitler . . . out of a sense of things so profoundly anti-Semitic as to the set the mind reeling'?

If the suspicion, however, still lingers that it was only the fact that the massacres in the Hebrew Bible were carried out by Jews that so troubled Weil, one should recall that from her earliest days she stood apart both by her refusal to overestimate the importance of time and by the direct physical impact made on her by the suffering of others. 'I remember when, in our youth', says Schumann, 'she suffered physically from discovering in Thucydides that the Athenians had, for example, sold the women and children of the Melians as slaves after having cut off the right hand or the left hand of the male Melians; she suffered physically from this knowledge for entire days.'[41] Is it any wonder that such a sensibility would react as Weil did to the stories of massacre that pile up in the Hebrew Bible which, sad to say, many readers find it so easy to 'pass over in silence'?

And yet did not Weil herself, it is often said, pass over in silence the holocaust that actually surrounded her? '[D]id you not have any thoughts', asks Sylvie Weil of her aunt, 'in any case not a word for all the Jewish babies crazed with terror, so cruelly separated from their mothers?'[42] What exactly is the thought here, however? That Simone, of all people, *didn't care* about the deaths of Jewish children? That it was all the same to her if they were ripped from the arms of their mothers and sent off to concentration camps? 'Simone Weil had learned from Dr Kac in January, 1943', writes Jacques Cabaud,[43] 'the fate that the Nazis had decided for the Jews. He was surprised that she did not react to the news that he had just told her.' One can learn a great deal from Cabaud's own reaction to this story. '[T]his genocide of a minority', he writes, 'could not have surprised her. She knew all too well what a spirit of exclusion could have in store for a group that finds itself as the scapegoat for public discontent.' Indeed. It is well to recall what she wrote to Georges Bernanos about her experiences in the Spanish Civil War: 'when once a certain class of people has been placed by the temporal and spiritual authorities outside the ranks of those whose life has value, then nothing comes more naturally to men than murder.'[44]

How, indeed, is one *supposed* to react to the kind of news delivered to Simone Weil by Dr Kac? 'With the news of a humanitarian disaster on the scale of the Holocaust, different personalities react differently', writes Cabaud.[45] 'As for Pius xii, he "exploded in sobs"'. Simone Weil, according to Dr Kac, '"became like a wall" in her silence. Here I see a sign that, far from being surprised, she had foreseen this ending.' There is a silence of indifference, and a silence of sadness beyond words. Is it really clear that it is the first that should be attributed to Simone Weil? Which silence, one must ask in turn, is to be attributed to those who quietly pass over the stories of little children ripped out of the arms of their mothers in the ancient massacres that fill up the Bible?

Can one really condemn Simone Weil, then, for the discomfiting questions she has raised about the Hebrew Bible? 'Saints are not given to us for the sake of comfort', said her wise friend, Thibon. Perhaps one can, after all, explain, or 'explain away', in some fashion those passages that so troubled Weil as historical reminders, say, of an ancient tradition that gradually developed in a different direction. But that would constitute more of a confirmation than a refutation of Weil's concerns. Weil herself, it should be noted, believed that as a Christian (of sorts) she needed to explain, *to distance herself* from certain passages in the Gospels – not to say, in the blood-stained history of the Church. Her testimony, however, is, as we have seen, that she searched in vain to find a priest who could account for the troubling passages in the Hebrew Bible *without endorsing* what she viewed as murders – albeit ancient ones. Is it any wonder she hesitated to join such a Church?

Yet it was not all of the Hebrew Bible from which Weil wished to distance herself. There are a number of passages that she adored – and the term is chosen advisedly. In *Letter to a Priest,* her list includes 'Isaiah, Job, the Song of Solomon, Daniel, Tobias, Part of Ezekiel, part of the Psalms, part of the Books of Wisdom, the Beginning of Genesis'.[46] She calls this list 'small' – no doubt impressed by the sheer volume of the passages she deplores (there are an awful lot of massacres) – and others have taken up the hint and used it as an excuse to downplay the significance of her list. Yet surely a selection from the Hebrew Bible that includes the Prophets, the Psalms, Job and Genesis can hardly be called insignificant. And Weil *loved* the passages she marked out. She could never praise too highly the book of Job – about which she wrote endlessly – which she called 'a pure marvel of truth and authenticity from beginning to end'.[47] She was shattered, as we saw earlier, by some words in Isaiah – 'They that love God shall run and not be weary', which she believed 'make it impossible for me to forget, even for a moment, that I am not of their number'.[48] She held that 'all the parts of the Old Testament in which the universal inspiration [the 'impersonal inspiration of God'] of antiquity has penetrated spread this conception before us *clothed in language of incomprehensible splendour.*'[49] She lamented the failure of the Christian tradition to attend to the world's beauty, which she considered the very signature of God: '[T]he beauty of the world is almost absent from the Christian tradition . . . [I]ndeed, there is little mention of the beauty of the world in the Gospel.'[50] She drew attention, however, to the fact that the parts of the Hebrew Bible she loved 'contain an incomparable expression of the beauty of the world.'[51]

Simone Weil, in short, *deplored the massacres* but *loved the beautiful passages* in the Hebrew Bible. This is anti-Judaism? She refused to believe that what inspired the massacre of Jericho could have been the same spirit that breathed life into the Sermon on the Mount. This is anti-Judaism? She denied that the worldview that guided the Book of Job could have been inscribed on the banner of conquest that flew over the 'army of the Lord.' Is this really anti-Judaism? Was she mistaken that the parts of the Hebrew Bible she admired were consonant with the Gospels – with the idea that God is essentially good – and that what lay behind those passages more closely resembled what had inspired Plato and Homer than what led to the slaughters contained in other parts of the Old Testament?

On the other hand, her historical speculations about the 'true origin' of her favoured parts of the Hebrew Bible are just that – speculations of an historical nature, the persuasiveness of which (or lack thereof) does not affect the force of her theological, her moral observations. Still, it is worth reminding ourselves that Freud, in *Moses and Monotheism*,[52] like Weil, speculated that the Hebrew Bible that has come down to us sprang from at least two different sources, one, Moses and Egyptian theology, the other, the warlike tradition of Yahweh. Like Weil, his speculations took place during the war with Nazi Germany, and as with her, he was roundly criticized for his supposed anti-Semitism. Contemporary biblical scholarship, of course, distinguishes a variety of different sources for the material contained in the Hebrew Bible, known today as the J, E, P and D texts.[53] Was Weil so far off the mark, then, even in her speculations of an historical nature, that different worldviews underlie different parts of the Hebrew Bible?

Yet a nagging concern still lingers. Should Weil really have launched her critique of the Jewish Bible at the very moment when the Jewish people were being massacred by the Nazis? Her actions do, however, have a precedent. Was it not Jesus himself who chose the very moment when the Jewish nation was being hounded by the Romans to launch into his critique of 'his own people' – which in this case, really was his own? (Note: they killed him.) And was it not Socrates who chose the very moment when Athens was caught in the embrace of a bloody war with Sparta to launch his assault on Athenian democracy? (Note: they killed him.) One can do worse than to be preceded in one's actions by Socrates and Christ.

Weil's actions, however, were in one respect very different. Her comments were not declaimed in the public marketplace like those of Christ and Socrates, for all to hear, nor published, like Freud's.

They were contained in letters to friends or in her private note-books, though a few dangerous remarks did, it is true, escape into essays intended for publication. It should be asked, however, when exactly it would be an appropriate time to criticize the Hebrew Bible. Today, when Israel, having survived countless wars, faces the possibility of nuclear annihilation? When, after all, in over two thousand years of persecution, has the nation of Israel not suffered from a mortal threat? Is one compelled, therefore, forever to 'pass over in silence' the troubling passages in the Hebrew Bible?

There is, moreover, something deeply confused in taking Weil to task for choosing that very moment in history to revisit the Hebrew Bible, as well as Roman and other ancient history. It was not *in spite of* but rather *because of* the Holocaust taking place around her that Weil looked to the ultimate cause of that world historical disaster. Like Karl Popper in *The Open Society and its Enemies*, she realized that the tragedy could not be attributed merely to the peculiarity of a people, the Germans, who had a taste for genocide. Like Popper, she considered it her duty to find the real origins of the neo-tribalism that was engulfing the modern world, the neo-collectivism, the preoccupation with race, with racial destiny, with being the unique people chosen by fate, God or history to teach the world its lessons at the point of a sword. Racial destiny; Chosen People; collective thinking; an army of conquest – it did not take a genius to recall those passages from the Hebrew Bible – the very passages that, as we have seen (see reference 26), George Steiner, who hurls anathemas at Weil, himself evoked in the concluding speech of his novel, *The Portage to San Cristóbal of A. H.*, a speech which Steiner refused to dis-avow. It did not require a genius, or an anti-Semite, to realize that when, through a quirk of history, Christianity – the religion of slaves – courtesy of Constantine and the Roman Empire, came to rule the world at the point of a sword, it was not the Gospels that were nailed to its banner.

What Weil can be held to account for, however, is to have generalized from her thoughtful critique of the Hebrew Bible to a thoughtless castigation of an entire culture, not to mention a great heritage. Preoccupied with passages that tormented her beyond words – especially since she believed deeply that they bore no little responsibility, via their influence, together with Rome, for the fact that the Church through the millennia turned itself into a worldly empire – she herself became guilty of creating caricatures of civili-zations, of Rome no less than Israel. (She is not alone in this, of course. There are not a few who, after the last world war, turned their back on everything German, forgetting that the same culture that produced Hitler gave us Beethoven and Goethe.)

She neglected her own cautionary advice in *Letter to a Priest* that 'a religion can only be known from the inside'.[54] She consulted priests, to be sure, but these, too, are outsiders; did she ever think to engage in discussion with a rabbi? She read the Church Fathers, studied St John of the Cross, but did she ever ponder the volumes of Maimonides and Rashi? Did she take a peek at the Talmud? What she found in the Hebrew Bible is indeed there, but was she sufficiently aware that there is more to the religion than that?

Sylvie Weil is thus justified in reminding her aunt about what she is missing when she recounts central European folk tales of rabbis whose generosity is the stuff of legend. 'I so regret', she writes, 'that Simone never read these tales, for the concept of charity is at the heart of Judaism. The duty of compassion towards the other is the most important of all.'[55] She alludes to 'amusing discussions between rabbis' that deal with such questions as, 'what is worse, or better, to be naked or to be hungry?' Simone, she says, 'steered clear of the Talmud, and I think she would have felt only contempt for such pedestrian discussions.' On the con-trary, surely. Could Simone Weil really have held any discussion about nakedness or hunger to be beneath her? It is not difficult to imagine her wrapped up in such a debate. For her part, however, she would surely at some point have wished to engage her niece in a different dialogue concerning her ancestral religion.

But Simone, sadly, died far too young for any such discussion to have taken place. Had she lived longer, would she have been open to enlightenment about what she had missed in the religion of her ancestors as it is actually lived by those who profess it? Her niece, in the course of time, moved into the house which Simone was only able to view from outside. The view from inside, Simone would have discovered, is very different. Could she have let her niece be her guide? 'You did something my sister would have ended up doing', said André Weil to his daughter, 'for she was honest, by and large.'[56]

9

The Crucifixion Suffices

> Armour, like the sword, is made of metal . . . If we want to have a love
> which will protect the soul from wounds, we must love something
> other than God.
> Simone Weil

The shock of Weil's reconsideration of the Hebrew Bible has given
rise to endless recriminations. It is matched, however, by her reimagination of the Gospels. '[I]f the Gospel omitted all mention of
Christ's resurrection', she writes to Father Couturier, 'faith would
be easier for me. The Cross by itself suffices.'[1] That this too can be
described as heresy is clear.[2] What is not immediately clear is what
she means by this remark, nor whether the truth (if not the Church)
is on her side. Weil's radical ideas, however, spring from a modest
source, her decision to take seriously the idea of *the incarnation of
the divine*. Her conclusions raise disturbing questions about the
self-understanding of Christians, but paradoxes arise also from her
own attempt, carrying forward a tradition as old as St Augustine,
to marry Christianity to Platonism.

'Now that Simone Weil has taught me how to read Plato', said
Wittgenstein's friend, M. O'C. Drury, 'I would bite my tongue out
rather than make [my earlier] remark, that . . . when Plato talks
about the gods, it lacks that sense of awe which you feel throughout
the Bible.'[3] For Weil, the true intersection, the centre of the cross,
lies where the road from Athens meets the one from Jerusalem.

Her Christianity is infused with Platonism, just as Platonism, for her, is a prefiguration of the Gospels. And yet was it Plato himself whom Weil embraced, or was she attached only to what has been called 'ethical Platonism'? To the editors of a recent volume on Weil, in agreement with the contribution by Michel Narcy, 'what counts most often as "Platonism" . . . the Theory of Ideas – is not at all what Weil was most interested in.'[4] Rather, on this view, 'for [Weil], Plato was a mystic . . . and [her] interest in Plato was in "ethical Platonism".'[5] One must be careful here, however. It is true that Weil saw Plato as a mystic and evinced no interest in scholarly debates on the Theory of Ideas or Forms. But she lacked interest as well in scholarly debates on the Bible, not to say, Homer, and yet her Bible was not at all the 'metaphysics-free' version constructed by Thomas Jefferson, for whom the good book was primarily a lesson in ethics, absent ontology – i.e. belief in a divine being.[6] Similarly, for Michael Wyschogrod, although 'the ethical is central in the deepest layers of Jewish consciousness', there is more to the Jewish Bible than ethics: 'ethical Judaism', he says, '[is] housebroken Judaism'.[7]

One can agree that Weil aligned herself with 'the Platonism that concerns itself with knowing the Good'.[8] Can one speak of the Good, however, in Plato's sense, without invoking his Ideas or Forms, of which, as he makes clear in the *Republic*, the Good is by far the most important? What exactly are these Forms? They are, one might say, 'perfections', and Weil speaks approvingly of what she calls the 'argument from perfection' or 'the ontological proof [of the existence of God], the certainty that *the perfect is more real than the imperfect*'.[9] Is this merely 'ethical Platonism'? As with Plato, one cannot, in the case of Weil, separate out the metaphysics from the ethics and the mysticism. 'The church may be ugly', she writes, 'the singing out of tune, the priest corrupt, and the faithful inattentive. In a sense that is of no importance.'[10] And why is that? As with Plato, she points to the example of mathematics, rightly understood.

'It is as with a geometrician who draws a figure to illustrate a proof. If the lines are not straight and the circles not round it is of no importance. Religious things are pure by right . . . [T]heir purity is unconditioned. No stain can sully it. That is why it is perfect.' Perfect, yes, but is it real? 'It is not . . . perfect in the same way as Roland's mare, which, while it has all possible virtues, had also the drawback of not existing . . . This virtue is unconditioned and perfect, and at the same time real.'

Weil, clearly, does not hesitate to go down the path laid by Plato, for whom each perfection, each Form or Idea, is, as the philosopher Richard Sharvy puts it, a kind of 'first cause'. Thus 'the many beautiful things in this world [are] beautiful because they participate in Beauty Itself, which is beautiful. But Beauty Itself must be beautiful in itself . . . indeed, *perfectly* beautiful . . . [and] not in virtue of any relation that it bears to anything else that is beautiful.'[11] Ontologically speaking, with a Platonic Form or Idea it can be said: the buck stops here. True, Weil holds that the moral of the famous allegory of the cave in Plato's *Republic*, a dialogue she never tires of quoting, is that the only way to attain to the ultimate reality of the Form of the Good is through a turn of the soul toward love, but love itself, she believes, as we have seen, 'is not consolation; it is light'[12] – Plato's own favourite metaphor for the epistemology of the Forms[13] – and 'sight is then the faculty which is in relationship with the good'.[14] Sight, clearly, is not a mere introspective feeling; what we see are things that are 'out there'. If they were not there, we would not see them. Mysticism, thus, for Weil, constitutes a heightened form of perception. As Marie Cabaud Meaney says, '[for Weil,] love is not only a lens sharpening our sight, it is the very organ of sight:[15] *L'amour est le regard de l'âme'.*[16] It is thus no surprise that Weil states that 'to desire truth is to desire direct contact with a piece of reality', and that 'to desire contact with a piece of reality is to love'.[17]

The question of Weil's commitment to full-blooded Platonism cannot, thus, be dismissed. What also cannot be passed over is the question of the consistency of Platonism, whether hers or Plato's, with what Weil recognizes as the fundamental idea of Christianity, the incarnation of the divine. To fully understand Simone Weil, then, one must go a little more deeply into Plato's philosophy. Basic to Plato's idea of the Forms is the concept of 'separation'. The Forms are transcendent, not immanent, 'reflected' by the particular instances in this world in which they 'participate', but never fully instantiated.[18] These Forms, one might say, borrowing an image from Newton,[19] operate by a kind of 'ontological action-at-a-distance'. It is the sheer beauty of the Beautiful, the goodness of the Good, that enables things that reflect their borrowed light to share their name and substance. And yet is not the idea of the incarnation of the divine precisely a conception of *divine immanence*, of God being, unlike the Forms – and, one might add, unlike the transcendent God of the Hebrew Bible – in some sense fully present 'on earth'? 'Heaven coming down to earth', says Weil, 'lifts earth to heaven.' That's the charm of it, but at the same time, there's the problem.

Is there a way to resolve this tension between Platonic transcendence and Christian immanence? If not, Weil was simply on the wrong track. What, however, if she is right that 'the essential property of God is that he is good'? Perhaps if the Form of the Good were to have its own peculiar features, there would be a chance for the Platonist. But the Good does stand apart from the other Forms, as Plato makes clear in the *Republic*. Is it different, however, in a way that will serve the purposes of the Christian Platonist? Perhaps, but to see this, one must invoke another great philosopher: Kant. Kant, though not a Platonist, shares with Plato the idea that the world around us, what he calls the world 'as it appears', does not represent reality as it is 'in itself'.[20] He agrees with Plato, however, that nevertheless we can sometimes touch reality. But where? Not via our reason. Kant, in spite of being a child of the Enlightenment, with its overestimation of the intellect, believes that it is only in virtue of our moral lives, our attachment to goodness, that we can reach ultimate reality. The pure will, he says, and it alone, is directly, literally capable of attaining goodness, and if it does so attain it, then it, the good will, is truly good in itself. The possibility thus opens up of a pure life, a just life, a life immaculately good which would not only *reflect* the divine Goodness, but *embody* it. The incarnation of the divine, Christ, on this conception, or Socrates, or Krishna, or whoever lived such a life, would be not merely, as it were, *the Mozart of Goodness* – a great reflection of something essentially transcendent, like the Beautiful – but Goodness itself, so to speak, become man; heaven come down to earth.

Weil's attempt to marry Platonism to Christianity was not after all misbegotten. Kant, it turns out, is the necessary middleman, and Weil provides a quote from Plato that serves as a bridge between Christianity and Kant: 'God is never in any way unrighteous. He is righteous to the supreme degree and nothing resembles him more than that man among us who is the most righteous.'[21] She is right to conclude, therefore, that for Plato 'the ideal model for relatively just men can only be a perfectly just man. Relatively just men exist. If their model is to be real, he must have an earthly existence at a certain point in space, and at a certain time.'[22] Abstraction is not enough. Philosophy stands in need of theology: 'one must be careful to notice how Plato clearly affirms that justice [as an abstraction] in itself is not a sufficient model. The model of justice for men is a just man.'[23]

The conclusion is inescapable. 'The passage [in Plato]', says Weil, 'concerning the perfectly just man demonstrates the idea of divine incarnation.'[24] Yet it must be noted that even if the possibility of incarnation that Weil is pointing to were realized, there is no guarantee that we would recognize it. We have been talking ontology – that is, being – not epistemology – knowing.[25] And history teaches us, with considerable help from Plato and Simone Weil, that it is precisely the good life, the just life, that is most difficult to recognize. Recall only that Socrates was poisoned and Jesus nailed to a cross; Joan of Arc burned alive; Gandhi and Martin Luther King Jr gunned down in their tracks. We have an eye, paradoxically, not for the Good, but for the Beautiful, the realm of 'aesthetics', of the senses. Yet it is only by our reflecting on the image given to us by the senses that the 'transcendent model' (in Weil's words[26]) of that image is revealed. 'Absolute beauty', she writes, 'is something as concrete as sensible objects, something which one sees, but sees by supernatural sight.'[27]

The Good itself, in contrast, may actually walk among us, yet our eyes are not made to see it. Sight alone – our natural faculty – will never discover what, as Gerard Manley Hopkins says, 'nor mouth had, no nor mind expressed, what heart heard of, ghost guessed'.[28] 'Beauty itself', says Weil, 'is the Son of God. For he is the image of the Father, and the Beautiful is the image of the Good.'[29] Insofar, that is, as the Son of God makes visible the invisible presence of the Father, he is, so to speak, playing the role of the Beautiful in relation to the Good – indeed, playing the role of the Son. But insofar as the Son is 'consubstantial' (*homoousian*), of the same substance as the Father, as stated in the Nicene Creed, God himself is present when his Son is. Indeed, that is precisely the doctrine of the incarnation of the divine.

But images can deceive, and there is wisdom in Plato's 'banishing the artists' in his *Republic*, as there is, as Kant insisted, in the prescription against graven images in the Hebrew Bible. For it is not because Plato underestimates the value of the beautiful that he makes his recommendation. On the contrary. 'Plato', says Iris Murdoch in *The Fire and the Sun: Why Plato Banished the Artists*, 'wants to cut art off from beauty, because he considers beauty too serious a matter to be commandeered by art.'[30] Man himself, after all, we are told in the Bible, is an 'image of God', but one made by God, not man. And in Christian theology, of course, Christ is an image of God, the reflection of a father in his son. In art, then, man imitates the very activity of God, and that, as Murdoch says, Plato considers too serious a business to relinquish to those who do not embrace the knowledge of God, that is to say, of the Good; i.e., for Plato, to those who are not philosophers.

And yet paradoxically, for Weil, nothing is more important than providing a way for God to 'enter into us', and no point of entry surpasses that of the Beautiful. The only other openings, she says, are affliction and the pure theoretical knowledge of science,[31] and yet 'those who have never felt [beauty] cannot perhaps be brought to God by any other path'.[32] Beauty is a trap: 'the soul's natural inclination to love beauty', she says, 'is the trap God most frequently uses in order to win it [over]'.[33]

It remains, however, that for Weil, despite the importance of beauty, the incarnation is a question of goodness, of a perfectly just life, something she insists is possible only for an individual. A nation cannot be perfectly just; it can never be holy. '[I]t is pos-sible for a man to attain such a degree of holiness that it is no longer he who lives, but Christ in him. Whereas, *there is no such thing as a holy nation*.'[34] She is thus in conflict with those who idolize Joan of Arc and the 'extreme patriots' who invoked her name to support their belief that de Gaulle represented the nation chosen by God. Yet 'France is not God, not by a long chalk.'[35] And this is no less true of Israel, despite its claim to represent 'the Chosen People'. Here Weil comes up against those who attempt to reconcile incar-nation with the idea of the Chosen.

In contrast, in a bold essay 'A Jewish Perspective on Incarnation', Michael Wyschogrod suggests that the possibility of incarnation cannot be ruled out, a priori, on Jewish grounds. Those who maintain otherwise, he asserts, are 'substituting a philosophical scheme for the sovereignty of God'.[36] Who are we, he suggests, to set a limit on what God could do, if he chose to? And yet, for Wyschogrod, it remains that Israel is 'the nation God [has de facto] elected', and thus, 'if we take the Hebrew Bible seriously, there cannot be any individual, however significant and prominent, whose relationship with God is unilateral, with the people of Israel not being the decisive presence serving as the purpose of the relation.'[37] And thus, for Wyschogrod, 'if the Church found God in this Jewish flesh [Jesus]', then perhaps, 'this was possible because God is in all Jewish flesh, because . . . it is the flesh of a people to whom God has attached himself.'[38]

Just this Weil would reject. We need to invoke the *Euthyphro* once more. If the Jewish people are chosen, it is *because* they were elected by God; he did not elect them *because* they were the chosen people. Being chosen is thus an *extrinsic* property, acquired by standing in a relationship to someone else, whereas being holy, being perfectly just, is an *intrinsic* property possessed by the bearer himself. Weil's point, then, contra Wyschogrod, remains: if a life like Christ's is indeed holy, it is not in virtue of the individual's relationship to a people.

And yet this very fact, surely, should have led Weil to rethink her critique. With the distinctions in mind that are made in the *Euthyphro*, Weil should acknowledge the possibility that a nation could be the 'chosen' one, in the sense of chosen by God to carry out a vital task. The mission to be accomplished might be holy, insofar as it is commanded by God, but not necessarily the nation chosen for the task. To be sure, there would naturally, perhaps unavoidably, be a temptation to turn what is chosen into an idol, but then it is perhaps also inevitable that one turn the incarnation of the divine in Christianity into an excuse for idolatry.[39] It is to be regretted, therefore, that Weil was moved to say that 'the Hebrews took for their idol not something made of metal or wood, but a race, a nation', and that 'their religion is essentially inseparable from such idolatry, because of the notion of the "chosen people"'.[40]

To be sure, the notion of being 'chosen' has long been debated within Judaism itself. Indeed, as the distinguished Jewish scholar Arthur Green has written, 'any sense that Christian exclusivism [has] been inherited from our claims of unique chosenness as God's only people [has been too often] dismissed [by Jews] as a cruel way of "blaming the victim".'[41] Nevertheless, Weil's complaint goes too far. A temptation, a tendency (toward idolatry or exclusivism), is one thing; it is something else to speak, as Weil has, of an 'essential inseparability'.

Whatever Wyschogrod's views, however, of the relationship of the incarnation to the Jewish people, it remains that he has taken the courageous stand of declaring that for Jews, it is not the possibility but only the actuality of incarnation that is the sticking point. Yet if one opens a door, one must be prepared to step through it. If Jews, or anyone else, reject the suggestion that the life of Jesus (or Socrates or Osiris) is an actualization of this possibility, what is it, one must ask, that such a life is lacking that excludes it from the requisite holiness? From a Jewish perspective, one is tempted to mention the obvious fact that Christ could not have been the awaited Messiah, since he did not, after all, free the Jewish people from Roman bondage, as Moses had led the Israelites out of Egypt. '[R]edemption from foreign domination', as Wyschogrod says, 'was almost a defining characteristic of the Messiah.'[42] Yet as he also points out, the question before us is not Messiah but God. But for this very reason it's unclear what aspects of holiness are lacking in the life of Christ. One cannot help feeling that in spite of his conceptual clarification, what appears to be missing for Wyschogrod is the power of the awaited Messiah, the ability to free one's people, to destroy one's enemies, to build up a great nation. De Gaulle, Weil might wryly note, satisfied these criteria for 'holy France' far more than Christ did for Israel.

Here, the two traditions do seem to clash. 'The false God', says Weil, 'changes suffering into violence. The true God changes violence into suffering.'[43] Each year, at Passover, Jews around the world celebrate God's having changed their suffering in Egypt into the violence brought down on the head of Pharaoh. Moses, with God's help, brings violence to the worshippers of the golden calf; Joshua, with the assistance of Jahweh, massacres the city of Jericho; and so on. The Hebrew Bible is filled with such stories. Can such a tradition recognize as divine the life of a 'loser', like Christ, who, in the process of getting himself killed, freed no one?

And yet there are elements of the Hebrew Bible that breathe an entirely different spirit. 'This is the word of the Lord', sayeth the prophet. 'Not by might, nor by power, but by My spirit.'[44] For the prophet, it is a question of justice: 'But the Lord of hosts shall be exalted in justice, The Holy One of Israel sanctified in righteousness.'[45] And what of the book of Job, where it is the righteous man himself who suffers? For Weil, as we have seen, these passages from the Hebrew Bible do speak with the same voice as the Gospels, but for that very reason, to her mind, they demonstrate that they spring from a different source. (Those sceptical of Weil might want to ask themselves whether one can celebrate Passover while repeating, with a straight face, 'not by might, nor by power'.) Whatever the force of her reasoning, it is not Weil, in the end, who can find no way to reconcile what is found in the Hebrew Bible with the meaning Christians discover in the Gospels. If Wyschogrod is listening to the prophets, attending to Job, what exactly does he believe is missing, one asks again, in the life story of the suffering Christ?

And yet, if Weil is right, there is an equal burden placed on Christians, on the human institution of the Church. For Christians celebrate as the capping stone of their religion the rebirth of Christ – the Resurrection. 'If Christ is not risen', says St Paul, 'all is in vain.'[46] Even Wittgenstein, whose love of the Gospels did not extend to St Paul, confessed that, 'what inclines even me to believe in Christ's Resurrection? . . . If he did not rise from the dead, then he decomposed in the grave like any other man. In that case, he is [merely] a teacher like any other and can no longer *help*; and once more we are orphaned and alone.'[47]

It is not a question, we must remind ourselves, of the *fact* of the Resurrection, but of its *meaning*. It is certainly heresy, but would it be correct to claim that in its insistence on the centrality of the Resurrection, the Church is being, paradoxically, 'too Jewish'? It is still looking for the Messiah, someone who, as Wittgenstein says, though dead, can still 'help us'; someone with influence or power. A distinction, however, must be made between Christ 'helping' us, in Wittgenstein's sense, and his life 'saving' ours. The coming of the Messiah, it could be said, changes everything, whereas 'God', according to Weil, 'changes nothing whatsoever.'[48] For her, Christ saves us by his very existence, by his having lived a perfectly just life, even if that life ended at the Crucifixion. 'The love we devote to the dead', she says, 'is perfectly pure . . . We desire that the dead man should have existed – and he has existed.'[49]

Right or wrong,[50] for Weil what is essential to Christianity is Christ's weakness,[51] not his strength, his death, not his resurrection. Yet, as she says, 'we die for what is strong, not for what is weak.'[52] Is this not why Christianity is, or ought to be, so *difficult* to accept? To borrow Neils Bohr's famous words about quantum mechanics, could it not be said that if Weil is right, those who are too easily prepared to accept Christianity have not really understood it?

This is the reasoning behind Weil's claim, which drove to distraction the priests she consulted, that 'the death on the Cross is something more divine than the Resurrection.'[53] It is not merely, for Weil, that those who insist on the centrality of the Resurrection are putting the emphasis in wrong place; rather, they are missing the very meaning of incarnation, and thus, 'today, the glorious Christ veils from us the Christ who was made a malediction'.[54] Ironically, it is all too often Christianity itself, as an institution, that stands between the believer and Christ, since '[a]fter the Resurrection, the infamous character of his ordeal was erased by glory, and today, across twenty centuries of adoration, the degradation which is the very essence of the Passion is hardly felt by us.'[55]

If the crucifixion suffices, however, for his divinity, then Christ is simply weak, end of story, with no asterisk or silver lining that points to his super-powers after Resurrection. (Superman, let us recall, is a comic book character based originally on Nietzsche, not the Gospels. He started out as a villain, and only gradually transformed himself into the popular hero.) To pray to God for protection, for deliverance from one's enemies, is evidence, for Weil, not of faith but idolatry. 'If a Christian', she says, 'worships God with a heart disposed like that of a pagan of Rome in the homage rendered to the Emperor, that Christian is an idolator.'[56] It is not sufficient to aim one's prayers *at the right object*; one must direct them *in the right way*. 'Affliction', she writes, 'confers immense prestige so long as it is accompanied by strength.'[57] This explains why 'no tortures had any further terrors' for the early Christians, convinced of the glorious Resurrection.[58] Yet, 'when Christ had only been an absolutely pure being, as soon as misfortune overtook him, he was abandoned.'[59]

To be sure, it takes courage to die for a glorified God, for the Resurrected Christ. Infinitely more courage, however – and of a different kind – is needed to stand by the weak and the abandoned, stripped of prestige, whom no armour can protect. 'Only an earthly attachment', says Weil, 'can afford protection from the coldness of steel. Armour, like the sword, is made of metal. . . . If we want to have a love which will protect the soul from wounds, we must love something other than God.'[60] A similar sentiment, inverted, was expressed by Wittgenstein in the previous world war. 'During [that war]', he said, 'the Germans got Krups to make a steel, bomb proof container to convey the consecrated host to the troops in the front line. This was disgusting. It should have had no protection from human hands at all.'[61] (As Christ had no protection, Weil might have added.) And George Steiner, too, has sounded this note.

'In Jerusalem today', he writes, 'at the "Shrine of the Scrolls" . . . [where] some of the Dead Sea Scrolls [are kept] . . . [there is a] hidden hydraulic mechanism whereby the entire edifice can, in the event of shelling . . . be made to sink safely below ground. Such precautions are indispensable . . . But [they] are also a metaphysical and ethical barbarism.'[62]

A common thread: what is holy does not provide nor require armour. For too many Christians, however, the signature of Christ's divinity is his Resurrection, which gives him the power to 'help us' in this life, to protect us from wounds. If this is a mistake, however, wherein lies his divinity? Was not Weil, after all, a supernaturalist? Did not her friend Thibon say that, 'never have I felt the word supernatural to be more charged with reality than when in contact with her'?[63] Where, then, for Weil, are the miracles?

Her answer is clear. '[C]ompassion for the afflicted is an impossibility. When it is really found [as in the life of Christ] we have a more astounding miracle than walking on water . . . or even raising the dead.'[64] If Emily Dickinson can speak of 'finite infinity',[65] we can perhaps describe Christianity as Weil sees it as a kind of 'natural supernaturalism'. The miracle is that goodness – goodness itself, not merely its reflection or imitation – can exist 'on earth'. 'What is good is also divine', says Wittgenstein. 'Queer as it sounds, that sums up my ethics.'[66] To be sure, much of what passes for goodness is not the real thing. 'If you offer a sacrifice', writes Wittgenstein, 'and are pleased with yourself about it, both you and your sacrifice will be cursed.'[67] That you are pleased with yourself is not surprising. And 'it is [also] not surprising', as Weil says, 'that a man who should bread should give a piece to someone who is starving. What is surprising is that he should be capable of doing so with so different a gesture from that with which we buy an object.'[68] That is where the miracle, the supernatural, enters the picture. For 'almsgiving when it is not supernatural is like a sort of purchase. It buys the sufferer.'[69]

Soraya Broukhim as Simone Weil in *An Interview with Simone Weil*, directed by Julia Haslett, 2010.

For Weil, in short, 'the unique supernatural fact in this world is holiness [a just life] itself.'[70] The supernatural fact of Christianity, the incarnation of the divine, the life of Christ, for Weil, comes down to the holiness of a just life, a life of pure goodness. 'Christ's attitude on this subject', she writes, 'as far as I understand it, was that he ought to be recognized as holy because he was perpetually and exclusively performing good.'[71] For Weil, as a Christian, contra Wyschogrod, such a life is not only possible, it was actual. But is Weil a Christian, not to say a Catholic, if she rejects the Resurrection – even if it is not the event itself, but the role it plays in Church doctrine? And can she be a Christian in her belief that it is almost certain that other lives have resembled Christ's – that there have been multiple incarnations of the divine?

Yet how could she not have maintained those beliefs, if it was the pure justice of Christ's life that was the miracle? Cannot other lives also possess such justice? Does not the contrary view represent a kind of fetish for this one person, Jesus, a 'cult of personality'? 'At all events', says Weil, 'we do not know for certain that there have not been incarnations previous to that of Jesus, and that Osiris in

Egypt, Krishna in India were not of that number.'[72] Indeed, 'if a Hindu believes that . . . the Word was incarnate in Krishna . . . before being so in Jesus, by what right can he be refused baptism?'[73] Did she really need to hear from her long-suffering priests what the decision would be of 'the compatibility or incompatibility of each of [these] opinions with membership [in] the Church?'[74] And would her chances of acceptance have improved by her adding a final touch, her belief that 'the feelings of the so-called pagans for their statues were very probably the same as those inspired nowadays by the crucifix and the statues of the Virgin', and that 'even if they did happen to believe the divinity to be totally present in some stone or wood, they were sometimes right. Do we not believe that God is present in some bread and wine?'[75] Yet does this not say as much about the Church, the Catholic (if not catholic) Church, as about Weil's heresies?

'I do not see', she noted, 'how I can avoid the conclusion that my vocation is to be a Christian outside the Church.'[76] Though she practically assaulted with questions the poor priests who fell into her orbit, she never really knocked on their front door. For Weil, one cannot even beg for entrance. 'The attitude that brings about salvation', she wrote, 'is not like any form of activity.'[77] One must become, rather, 'the slave who waits near the door so as to open it immediately when the master knocks'. The slave who, 'even if he is told the master is dead, and even if he believes it . . . will not move'. This, she said, is 'the best image [of salvation]'.[78] Is it not also a representation of Weil's own life? Forever outside, she spent a lifetime waiting to be invited in. If the call never came, who is to say there was not another door that beckoned?

References

Introduction

1 Sylvie Weil, *Chez les Weil: André et Simone* (Paris, 2009).
2 Simone Weil, *Gravity and Grace*, trans. E. Craufurd (London, 1992), p. 22.
3 Ibid., pp. 132–3.
4 Simone Weil, *Intimations of Christianity among the Ancient Greeks* (London, 1987).
5 Peter Hebblethwaite, *The Year of the Three Popes* (London, 1978), p. 2.
6 Czeslaw Milosz, 'Nobel Lecture', 8 December 1980.
7 Czeslaw Milosz, *To Begin Where I Am* (New York, 2002).
8 Jacques Cabaud, *Simone Weil: A Fellowship in Love* (New York, 1964).
9 Simone Pétrement, *Simone Weil: A Life*, trans. R. Rosenthal (New York, 1976).
10 Francine du Plessix Gray, *Simone Weil* (New York, 2001).
11 Perhaps, as in the Banach-Tarski Paradox, Simone Weil's life can be taken apart and the pieces reassembled to form a figure of any size and shape we please. 'The Banach-Tarski Paradox . . . is often stated in the fanciful form: a pea may be taken apart into finitely many pieces that may be rearranged using rotations and translations to form a ball the size of the sun' (Stan Wagon, *The Banach-Tarski Paradox*, New York, 1993, pp. 3–4).
12 Weil, *Intimations of Christianity among the Ancient Greeks*, p. 92.
13 Simone Weil, *First and Last Notebooks*, trans. R. Rees (London, 1970), p. 171. Quoted by Marie Cabaud Meaney in *Simone Weil's Apologetic Use of Literature: Her Christological Interpretation of Ancient Greek Texts* (Oxford, 2007). As Meaney points out (p. 18), 'Weil's approach is the

polar opposite of positivism: rather than reducing reality to the empirical data gathered through sense perception, she sees the sacred . . . everywhere.'

14 Imre Lakatos, *Mathematics, Science and Epistemology* (Cambridge, 1987), p. 4.

15 Simone Weil, *The Notebooks of Simone Weil*, trans. A. Wills (New York, 1956), p. 370.

16 Wittgenstein, *Culture and Value*, trans. P. Winch (Chicago, 1984), p. 5.

17 Weil, *Gravity and Grace*, p. 11.

18 Weil, *Intimations of Christianity among the Ancient Greeks*, p. 82.

19 Why Golgotha? According to Steiner, Christianity has never forgiven Jews for what happened to Christ; the horrors of the twentieth century represent the full flowering of that resentment.

20 George Steiner, *No Passion Spent* (New Haven, CT, 1996).

21 Simone Weil, *On Oppression and Liberty*, trans. A. Wills and J. Patrie (Amherst, MA, 1973).

22 Weil, *Gravity and Grace*.

23 Karl Popper, *The Open Society and its Enemies* (London, 1963).

24 'The Roman Empire', said Hitler *(Hitler's Table Talk: 1941–1944*, trans. N. Cameron and R. H. Stevens, New York, 2000, p. 10), 'is a great political creation, the greatest of all . . . The smallest palazzo in Florence or Rome is worth more than all Windsor Castle. If the English destroy anything in Florence or Rome, it will be a crime. In Moscow, it wouldn't do any great harm; nor in Berlin, unfortunately . . .'

25 It should be noted that Nietzsche, whom Weil despised, in exact contrast to her, described (in *The Genealogy of Morals*, trans. W. Kaufman, New York, 1989) 'Rome v. Judea' as one of the 'great battles' of all time. Weil, for her part, acknowledged this great battle, but added her own observation that the very reason Judea could mount such a serious challenge to Rome was because it shared something of its warlike spirit.

26 Simone Weil, *Letter to a Priest*, trans. A. Wills (London, 1953), pp. 62–3.

27 Simone Weil, *The Need for Roots*, trans. A. Wills (London, 1987), p. 126.

28 In *Culture and Value*, for example, he writes that, 'among Jews, "genius" is found only in the holy man. Even the greatest of Jewish thinkers is no more than talented. (Myself, for instance.)' (p. 18). And there is more along this line of thought.

29 David Edmonds and John Eidinow, *Wittgenstein's Poker: The Story of a Ten-Minute Argument Between Two Great Philosophers* (New York, 2001), p. 108 and passim.

30 *Recollections of Wittgenstein*, ed. R. Rhees (Oxford, 1984), p. 86.

31 Simone Weil, *Seventy Letters*, trans. and ed. R. Rees (London, 1965), p. 175.

32 Robert Coles, *Simone Weil: A Modern Pilgrimage* (Reading, MA, 1987), p. xviii.

33 Sylvie Weil, *Chez Les Weil*.

34 Ibid., p. 30.

35 'Simone Weil against the Bible', p. 133, in Emmanuel Levinas, *Difficult Freedom: Essays on Judaism*, trans. S. Hand (Baltimore, MD, 1990).

36 Mary Warnock, ed., *Women Philosophers* (London, 1996).

37 Ibid., 'Introduction', p. xxxii.

38 Iris Murdoch, *The Sovereignty of Good* (London, 1985).

39 Iris Murdoch, *The Fire and the Sun* (New York, 1990).

40 Murdoch, *The Sovereignty of Good*, p. 50.

41 The almost total absence of actual arguments in the only book Wittgenstein published during his lifetime, the *Tractatus Logico-Philosophicus*, trans. D. F. Pears and B. F. McGuinness (London, 1974), drove his friend and mentor Bertrand Russell almost to distraction.

42 As he announces in the *Tractatus*.

43 To his friend Dury he once said, 'there is a sense in which you and I are both Christians' (*Recollections of Wittgenstein*, p. 114). Indeed, as will be seen later, in the trenches in the First World War he was known as 'the one with the Gospels', since he was never without a copy of Leo Tolstoy's stories from the Gospels in his knapsack. Like Weil, his turn toward Christian mysticism was as much a surprise to himself as to others.

44 '[According to Wittgenstein,] a human being should do the thing for which he has a talent with all his energy his life long, and should never relax his devotion to his job merely in order to prolong his existence. This *platonistic attitude* was manifested . . . [also] late . . .' (Norman Malcolm, *Ludwig Wittgenstein: A Memoir*, Oxford, 1984, p. 57; emphasis added).

45 *Recollections of Wittgenstein*, p. 98.

46 Among these will be the logician, Kurt Gödel, a colleague of Weil's brother, the mathematician André Weil, at Princeton's Institute for

Advanced Study (and like Weil, see n. 13, a crusader against Positivism), and, of course, Joan of Arc.

47 Meaney, *Simone Weil's Apologetic Use of Literature*.

48 *Recollections of Wittgenstein*, p. 117.

1 Three Simones

1 Three years older.

2 Yet Sylvie Weil says in 'The Stuffed Carp', *Chez Les Weil: André et Simone* (Paris, 2009), that neither would have considered marrying a non-Jew, or not being married by a rabbi.

3 'Return to Sources', ibid.

4 A contemporary French Jewish scholar. See Francine du Plessix Gray, *Simone Weil* (New York, 2001), p. 10.

5 German Foreign Minister in the Weimar Republic, an anti-Zionist who insisted that Germany fulfil the terms of the Treaty of Versailles, Walther Rathenau was assassinated on 24 June 1922. The Nazis would soon proclaim the assassins national heroes.

6 'That's why I'm such a failure.' See du Plessix Gray, *Simone Weil*, p. 7.

7 Later, however, she claimed to enjoy being kissed by men with moustaches, because 'it stings' (Jacques Cabaud, *Simone Weil: A Fellowship in Love*, New York, 1964, p. 19).

8 Du Plessix Gray, *Simone Weil*, p. 19.

9 Sylvie Weil, '*Kuckucksei's* Metamorphoses', *Chez Les Weil*.

10 As Sylvie Weil, ibid., has also emphasized.

11 See especially du Plessix Gray, *Simone Weil*.

12 Leslie Fiedler, Introduction, in Simone Weil, *Waiting for God*, trans. E. Craufurd (New York, 2001), p. xvi.

13 Jacques Cabaud, *Simone Weil: A Fellowship*, p. 19.

14 Du Plessix Gray, *Simone Weil*, p. 17.

15 Simone would recall 'falling into a bottomless pit of despair' at the age of fourteen when she compared her intellect to her brother's. Du Plessix Gray, *Simone Weil*, p. 17, notes, strangely, that this is an example of those feelings of 'extreme worthlessness common to most young anorexics'. But most young girls are not forced to compare themselves with a brother with the mind of Pascal!

16 Sylvie Weil, 'A Two Headed Genius', *Chez Les Weil*.

17 Du Plessix Gray, *Simone Weil*, p. 20.

18 Ibid., p. 25.

19 Simone Weil, *Intimations of Christianity among the Ancient Greeks* (London, 1987), p. 80. The quotation is from Plato's *Gorgias*, 523a.

20 Simone Weil, *Gravity and Grace*, trans. E. Craufurd (London, 1992), p. 82. Emphasis added.

21 The lawyer who drew up the deed which enabled Wittgenstein to forfeit his inheritance was shocked by the lengths to which the philosopher had gone to rule out any possibility of the fortune finding its way back to him. He had never seen such a document before.

22 Weil, *Gravity and Grace*, p. 29.

23 Simone Weil, *Waiting for God*, trans. E. Craufurd (New York, 2001), p. 105.

24 Jacques Cabaud, *Simone Weil: A Fellowship*, p. 17.

25 Simone Pétrement, *Simone Weil: A Life*, trans. R. Rosenthal (New York, 1976), p. 13.

26 Cabaud's adjective. As he put it, 'hers was a Roman soul', *Simone Weil: A Fellowship*, p. 19.

27 J. B. Perrin and G. Thibon, *Simone Weil as We Knew Her*, trans. E. Craufurd (London, 1953), p. 127.

28 Cabaud, *Simone Weil: A Fellowship*, p. 19.

29 Du Plessix Gray, *Simone Weil*, p. 39.

30 Jacques Cabaud, 'Was Simone Weil an Anti-Semite?', in *Simone Weil: Philosophe, Historienne, et Mystique*, ed. G. Kahn (Paris, 1978).

31 Perrin and Thibon, *Simone Weil as We Knew Her*, p. 122.

32 Weil, *Waiting for God*, p. 27.

33 Potok, *The Chosen* (New York, 1967), pp. 263–4.

34 *Recollections of Wittgenstein*, ed. R. Rhees (Oxford, 1984), p. 64.

35 Weil, *Gravity and Grace*, p. 13. Weil elsewhere made her point in a more gentle, if equally bleak way: 'The difference between more or less intelligent men', she wrote, 'is like the difference between criminals condemned to life imprisonment in smaller or larger cells' (*Selected Essays: 1934–43*, trans. R. Rees, London, 1962, p. 26).

36 Du Plessix Gray, *Simone Weil*, p. 15.

37 Sylvie Weil, 'A Two-Headed Genius', *Chez Les Weil*.

38 Perrin and Thibon, *Simone Weil as We Knew Her*, p. 118.

39 Palle Yourgrau, *A World Without Time: The Forgotten Legacy of Gödel and Einstein* (New York, 2005), p. 5: '"Snow White and the Seven Dwarfs" [was Gödel's] favourite movie. History does not record which of the seven dwarfs was Gödel's favourite, but we do know why he favored fairy tales: "Only fables", he said, "present the world as it should be and as if it had meaning".'

40 As Sylvie points out, in photographs of these meetings, while others are laughing, Simone is all business, wrapped up in intense scrutiny of her notes.

41 Sylvie Weil, 'A Two-Headed Genius', *Chez Les Weil*.

42 Du Plessix Gray, *Simone Weil*, p. 16.

43 Blake, *Poems of Innocence and Experience*. Interestingly, 'Blake', says Norman Malcolm, a friend and former student of Wittgenstein's, 'was one of [Wittgenstein's] favorite English poets; he quoted verses to [his friend] Drury from memory' (*Recollections of Wittgenstein*, p. xvi).

44 Du Plessix Gray, *Simone Weil*, pp. 229–31.

45 'His true Penelope was Flaubert,
He fished by obstinate isles;
Observed the elegance of Circe's hair
Rather than the mottoes on sun-dials.'
    Ezra Pound, 'Hugh Selwyn Mauberley'.

2 Six Swans

1 J. B. Perrin and G. Thibon, *Simone Weil as We Knew Her*, trans. E. Craufurd (London, 1953), p. 116.

2 Francine du Plessix Gray, *Simone Weil* (New York, 2001), p. 19.

3 Sylvie Weil, 'A Navy Blue Beret', *Chez Les Weil: André et Simone* (Paris, 2009).

4 Perrin and Thibon, *Simone Weil as We Knew Her*, p. 127.

5 Ibid., p. 127.

6 Sylvie Weil, 'A Navy Blue Beret'.

7 Jacques Cabaud, *Simone Weil: A Fellowship in Love* (New York, 1964), p. 127.

8 John Hellman, *Simone Weil: An Introduction to Her Thought* (Waterloo, ON, 1982), p. 19.

9 There is, however, always someone who tries to provide such a reductive account. Thus Roger Judrin: 'There is no student of Alain who, reading Simone Weil, doesn't feel that she owes almost everything to her master' (quoted by Maurice Schumann in 'Presentation of Simone Weil', trans. A. Fineman in *Simone Weil: Philosophe, Historienne, et Mystique*, ed. G. Kahn, Paris, 1978).

10 Quoted by Jacques Cabaud, in 'Introduction' to *Simone Weil: A Fellowship in Love*.

11 Nancy Huston, *Longings and Belongings* (Toronto, ON, 2005).

12 Du Plessix Gray, *Simone Weil*, p. 32.

13 Not by du Plessix Gray, who notes correctly that Weil's *topoi* 'foreshadow her entire spiritual development' (ibid., p. 32).

14 Simone Weil, *Intimations of Christianity among the Ancient Greeks* (London, 1987), p. 98.

15 'The world is all that is the case', begins Wittgenstein's *Tractatus*. 'It is the totality of facts.' As will be seen, with regard to 'questions of the spirit', there is a deep consonance between the ideas of Wittgenstein and Weil.

16 'The sense of the world', writes Wittgenstein in the *Tractatus*, 'must lie outside the world' (6.41).

17 Wittgenstein, *Culture and Value*, trans. P. Winch (Chicago, 1984), p. 3.

18 Simone Weil, *Gravity and Grace*, trans. E. Craufurd (London, 1992), p. 3.

19 On this point she will reproach her youthful hero, Pascal.

20 'We die for what is strong', she writes in *Gravity and Grace* (p. 22), 'not for what is weak.'

21 William Butler Yeats, 'The Wild Swans at Coole'.

22 Gerard Manley Hopkins, 'The Windhover (To Christ our Lord)'.

23 Cabaud, *Simone Weil: A Fellowship*, p. 333. 'The only punishment', says Weil, 'capable of [truly] punishing Hitler, and deterring little boys thirsting for greatness in coming centuries from following his example, is such a total transformation of the meaning attached to greatness that he should thereby be excluded from it' (*The Need for Roots*, trans. A. Wills, London, 1987, p. 217).

24 Hopkins, 'The Windhover'.

25 Du Plessix Gray, *Simone Weil*, p. 29.

26 Ibid., p. 74.

27 Both died young, more or less as suicides. Van Gogh at 37, from a gunshot to the head, Weil at 34, from tuberculosis exacerbated by starvation.

28 Du Plessix Gray, *Simone Weil*, p. 41.

29 Cabaud, *Simone Weil: A Fellowship*, p. 51.

30 Athanasios Moulakis, *Simone Weil and the Politics of Self-Denial*, trans. R. Hein (Columbia, MO, 1998), p. 85.

31 Du Plessix Gray, *Simone Weil*, p. 30.

32 Matthew 4:19. Gathering his disciples, Jesus finds Simon (or Simone?), called Peter, and Andrew casting their nets into the sea. 'Come with me', he says, 'and I will make you fishers of men.' (*Oxford NIV Scofield Study Bible: New International Edition*, New York, 1984).

33 Du Plessix Gray, *Simone Weil*, pp. 42–3.

34 Quoted by John Hellman, *Simone Weil: An Introduction to her Thought* (Waterloo, ON, 1982), p. 10.

35 Ibid., p. 7.

36 Simone de Beauvoir, *Memoirs of a Dutiful Daughter* (New York, 1974), quoted in du Plessix Gray, *Simone Weil*, p. 35.

37 Simone de Beauvoir, *The Prime of Life* (New York, 1973), quoted by Hellman, *Simone Weil*, p. 13.

38 Hellman, *Simone Weil*, p. 13.

3 *Au Revoir, La Révolution*

1 An observation that Sylvie Weil, too, cannot resist making in *Chez Les Weil: André et Simone* (Paris, 2009).

2 Jacques Cabaud, *Simone Weil: A Fellowship in Love* (New York, 1964), p. 53.

3 Wittgenstein, *Culture and Value*, trans. P. Winch (Chicago, IL, 1984), p. 14.

4 Simone Weil, *Lectures on Philosophy*, trans. H. Price (Cambridge, 1993).

5 Francine du Plessix Gray, *Simone Weil* (New York, 2001), p. 59.

6 Cabaud, *Simone Weil: A Fellowship*, p. 85.

7 Simone Weil, *Intimations of Christianity among the Ancient Greeks*

(London, 1987), p. 165.

8 As we will see later, W. Rabi, in a famous essay, will take Weil to task for failing to appreciate what he describes as the Jewish view, as opposed to Weil's, that salvation is essentially of the collective, of the people, of the Jewish people.

9 Du Plessix Gray, *Simone Weil*, p. 73.

10 Ibid., p. 76.

11 Jean van Heijenoort, *From Frege to Gödel: A Source Book in Mathematical Logic, 1879–1931* (Cambridge, MA, 1967).

12 Famous for revolution and logic, van Heijenoort was also a renowned lover, which led to his demise. Returning to Mexico City to attend to a disturbed former wife, he was shot to death by her while he lay in bed – rejoining thus his mentor, Trotsky, who had met with an even more violent death in Mexico (by ice pick, courtesy of Joseph Stalin). See Anita Feferman, *Politics, Logic and Love: The Life of Jean van Heijenoort* (Natick, MA, 1993).

13 Du Plessix Gray, *Simone Weil*, p. 70.

14 When one of his generals protested the excesses carried out by the German army during Operation Barbarossa, Hitler, according to his adjutant, Major Engel, complained about such 'childish' reactions, adding that 'one can't fight a war with Salvation Army methods'. (Laurence Rees, *The Nazis: A Warning from History*, New York, 1997, pp. 130–31.)

15 Simone Weil, 'Analysis of Oppression', p. 138, in *The Simone Weil Reader*, ed. G. Panichas (Wakefield, RI, 1977).

16 The two logicians who figure in the title of the volume put together by Trotsky's bodyguard, van Heijenoort, who accompanied Trotsky to the Weils, namely, Frege and Gödel, represent two lonely voices in the foundations of mathematics who believed that logic and mathematics will not be true sciences unless their axioms can be rationally justified (though obviously, not proved; you can't prove an axiom).

17 Weil, 'Analysis of Oppression', p. 144.

18 Ibid., p. 145 (emphasis added).

19 Ibid., p. 147.

20 Ibid., p. 151.

21 Du Plessix Gray, *Simone Weil*, p. 81.

22 Ibid., p. 100.

23 Simone Weil, *Seventy Letters*, trans. and ed. R. Rees (London, 1965), p. 44.
24 Du Plessix Gray, *Simone Weil*, p. 93. Is it possible to imagine Lenin or Trotsky allowing themselves to be thrown into a situation where they would be at the mercy of such scoldings?
25 Ibid., p. 85.
26 Ibid., p. 90.
27 Pascal, *Pensées*, trans. A. J. Krailsheimer (Harmondsworth, 1966), p. 425.
28 Quoted by C. S. Lewis in *The Problem of Pain* (San Francisco, CA, 1996), p. 94.
29 Weil, *Seventy Letters*, p. 170. Compare Wittgenstein: 'I am too soft, too weak, and so too lazy to achieve anything significant. The industry of great men is, among other things, a sign of their *strength* . . .' (*Culture and Value*, p. 72).

4 A Lesson in War

1 Jacques Cabaud, *Simone Weil: A Fellowship in Love* (New York, 1964), p. 15.
2 Simone Weil, *Gravity and Grace,* trans. E. Craufurd (London, 1992), p. 77.
3 Letter to Georges Bernanos, in Simone Weil, *Seventy Letters*, trans. and ed. R. Rees (London, 1965), p. 106.
4 R. Rhees, ed., *Recollections of Wittgenstein* (Oxford, 1984), p. 193.
5 Ibid., p. 194.
6 Ibid., p. 149.
7 Isaac Babel, *Red Cavalry*, trans. W. Morison (Cleveland, OH, 1960)
8 Francine du Plessix Gray, *Simone Weil* (New York, 2001), pp. 112–13.
9 Letter to Bernanos, p. 107.
10 Ibid., p. 109.
11 Ibid., p. 107.
12 Georges Bernanos, *Les Grands Cimetières sous la Lune* (Paris, 1997).
13 Simone Weil, Letter to Georges Berganos, p. 108.
14 Ibid., p. 109.
15 Weil, *Gravity and Grace*, p. 89.

16 Ibid., p. 63.

17 Ibid., p. 89.

18 Ibid., p. 91. 'Marxist dialectic', Weil adds, 'is based on a very degraded and completely warped view of this'.

19 Ibid., p. 92. It also helps explain the story of Abraham and Isaac, in which Abraham must struggle with his attachment to a particular thing, here below – his only son – and his very different attachment to God. See Marie Cabaud Meaney's penetrating discussion of Weil's 'Christological' study of *Antigone* in *Simone Weil's Apologetic Use of Literature: Her Christological Interpretation of Ancient Greek Texts* (Oxford, 2007).

20 As we have seen, she admires Bernanos for just this equity. In time, T. E. Lawrence will be added to this list: 'I read his *The Seven Pillars of Wisdom*', she writes to Jean Posternak, '. . . Never since the *Iliad*, as far as I know, has a war been described with such sincerity, with such a total absence of heroic rhetoric' (Du Plessix Gray, *Simone Weil*, p. 130).

21 Weil, 'The *Iliad*, Poem of Force', in *The Simone Weil Reader*, ed. G. Panichas (Wakefield, RI, 1994) (where it is translated, 'Poem of Might'), pp. 50–51.

22 Ibid., pp. 33–4.

23 Ibid., p. 35.

24 Ibid., p. 35. True, in Palle Yourgrau, *A World Without Time: The Forgotten Legacy of Gödel and Einstein* (New York, 2005), p. 18, one reads that 'western thought as such, one might say, is characterized by a kind of geometrical midas touch. Whatever science touches becomes subject to geometry.' Correctly understood, however, this serves to confirm Weil's point that 'we are only geometricians in regard to matter'. What Plato meant by geometry is a far cry from what it means today.

25 Weil, 'The *Iliad*, Poem of Force', p. 52.

26 Weil, *Gravity and Grace*, p. 101.

27 Weil, 'The *Iliad*, Poem of Force', p. 42.

28 Du Plessix Gray, *Simone Weil*, p. 118.

29 Simone Weil, *The Need for Roots*, trans. A. Wills (London, 1987), p. 89.

30 Du Plessix Gray, *Simone Weil*, p. 133.

31 Weil, *Seventy Letters*, p. 75.

32 Ibid., p. 85.

33 Simone Weil, *Waiting for God*, trans. E. Craufurd (New York, 2001), p. 26.

34 Weil, *Gravity and Grace*, p. 137.

5 A Great Day for Indo-China

1 Francine du Plessix Gray, *Simone Weil* (New York, 2001), p. 127.

2 Dubbed thus by Weil for the 'angelic radiance' emanating from him during communion.

3 She would also, naturally, have been sympathetic with John Donne. 'I need God to take me by force', she writes in *Gravity and Grace*, trans. E. Craufurd (London, 1992). 'Love is something divine', she also wrote, 'Once it invades the human heart, it will break it' (*La Connaissance Surnaturelle*, Paris, 1950). One is immediately reminded of John Donne's Holy Sonnet XIV: 'Batter my heart, three-person'd God . . . imprison me, for I, except you enthrall me, never shall be free.'

4 Jacques Cabaud, *Simone Weil: A Fellowship in Love* (New York, 1964), p. 170.

5 Du Plessix Gray, *Simone Weil*, p. 128.

6 As it was commonly referred to in Weil's day, but known today, less contentiously, as the Hebrew Bible, and with good reason. 'The Old Testament' suggests, unavoidably, a contrast (as in television commercials) with the 'New and Improved' Testament.

7 Du Plessix Gray, *Simone Weil*, p. 147.

8 Cabaud, *Simone Weil: A Fellowship*, p. 176. Weil had joined a discussion group organized around the journal, *Nouveaux Cahiers*.

9 It was only natural, then, that she would campaign actively for pacifism, a position she would soon come to regret. Interestingly, one of the 'mass meetings' of pacifists in which she participated, held at the Chateau de Moncel in Jouy-en-Josias, near Paris, in April 1938, was attended also by the legendary school reformer Maria Montessori.

10 *Plus ça change, plus ça reste la même chose*. When the First World War broke out, Bertrand Russell in England and Albert Einstein in Germany were horrified at the sudden, virulent nationalism that

sprang up among their erstwhile moderate colleagues, who were themselves outraged at Einstein's and Russell's failure to join them.

11 Simone Weil, '*The Iliad*: Poem of Might', in *Intimations of Christianity among the Ancient Greeks* (London, 1987), p. 24. 'Force' is here substituted for 'Might' in this translation.

12 Weil, *Gravity and Grace*, p. 59.

13 Ibid., p. 75.

14 Weil, 'The *Iliad*, Poem of Force', pp. 31–2.

15 Ibid., p. 35.

16 Ibid., p. 52.

17 Ibid., p. 53.

18 As we will see later, for this very reason, Weil suggests that the Book of Job must have originated in an alternate religious tradition.

19 Weil, 'The *Iliad*, Poem of Force', p. 54.

20 Cabaud, *Simone Weil: A Fellowship*, p. 166.

21 Ibid., p. 211.

22 Weil, 'The *Iliad*, Poem of Force', p. 54.

23 Ibid., p. 54.

24 Du Plessix Gray, *Simone Weil*, p. 147.

25 As indicated in reference 6 above, to refer to the Hebrew Bible as the Old Testament, without further explanation, is prejudicial. The explanation in the present context is that it is useful to employ the old appellations to bring out more clearly the respects in which the texts are 'parallel', the sense in which each text 'points to' the other.

26 Elaine Scarry, *The Body in Pain: The Making and Unmaking of the World* (New York, 1985).

27 Ibid., p. 184.

28 Ibid., p. 195.

29 Ibid., p. 213.

30 Ibid., p. 212.

31 Ibid., p. 214.

32 Simone Weil, *The Need for Roots*, trans. A. Wills (London, 1987), p. 48.

33 Simone Weil, *Venise Sauvé: Tragédie en Trois Actes* (Paris, 1955).

34 Jeffrey Mehlman, *Emigré New York: French Intellectuals in Wartime Manhattan, 1940–1944* (Baltimore, MD, 2000), pp. 90–91.

35 Weil, *The Need for Roots*, p. 41.

36 Ibid., p. 45.

37 Ibid., p. 49.
38 Ibid., p. 8.
39 Ibid., p. 137.
40 'Diary: Written by professor Dr Gottlob Frege in the time from 10 March to 9 April, 1924', trans. R. Mendelsohn, ed. G. Gabriel and W. Kienzler, *Inquiry*, 39 (1996).
41 Weil, *Gravity and Grace*, p. 149.
42 Weil, *The Need for Roots*, p. 150.
43 Ibid.
44 Ibid.
45 Ibid., p. 8.
46 Ibid., pp. 151–2.
47 Ibid., p. 125.
48 Weil, *Intimations of Christianity among the Ancient Greeks*, p. 174. Emphasis added.
49 Simone Weil, *Waiting for God*, trans. E. Craufurd (New York, 2001), p. 99.
50 Conor Cruise O'Brien, 'The Anti-Politics of Simone Weil', *New York Review of Books* (12 May 1977).
51 David Rieff, 'European Time', in *The New Salamagandi Reader*, ed. R. Boyers and P. Boyers (Syracuse, NY, 1996), p. 135.
52 Ibid., p. 136.
53 Ibid., pp. 136–7.
54 Ibid.
55 Ibid., p. 139.
56 Mehlman, *Emigré New York*, p. 88.
57 Rieff, 'European Time', p. 138.
58 Ibid.
59 Weil, *The Need for Roots*, p. 268.
60 Simone Weil, in *On Science, Necessity and the Love of God*, trans. R. Rees (London, 1968).
61 Ibid., pp. 54–5.
62 Ibid., p. 139.
63 René Thom, '"Modern" Mathematics: An Educational and Philosophic Error?', in *New Directions in the Philosophy of Mathematics*, ed. T. Tymoczko (Boston, MA, 1985), p. 77.
64 Du Plessix Gray, *Simone Weil*, p. 175.

65 Jacques Cabaud,'Was Simone Weil an Anti-Semite?', in *Simone Weil: Philosophe, Historienne, et Mystique*, ed. G. Kahn (Paris, 1978).

66 J. B. Perrin and G. Thibon, *Simone Weil as We Knew Her*, trans. E. Craufurd (London, 1953), p. 120.

67 Ibid., p. 125.

68 Ibid., p. 127.

69 Ibid.

70 Ibid., p. 136.

71 Ibid., p. 137.

72 Ibid., p. 138.

73 Ibid., p. 143.

74 Ibid., p. 153.

75 Ibid., p. 159.

76 Ibid. It should be clear from this that it is inappropriate for so many commentators to single out as 'the' reason for Weil's hesitations concerning baptism the fact that the Church continued to include the Hebrew Bible as a sacred text.

77 Du Plessix Gray, *Simone Weil*, p. 180.

6 A Difference between France and God

1 Jacques Cabaud, *Simone Weil: A Fellowship in Love* (New York, 1964), p. 272.

2 Ibid., p. 275.

3 Simone Weil, *The Need for Roots*, trans. A. Wills (London, 1987), p. 221.

4 Francine Du Plessix Gray, *Simone Weil* (New York, 2001), p. 182.

5 See 'Beat Up the Poor', in his *Paris Spleen*, trans. L. Varèse (New York, 1970).

6 Du Plessix Gray, *Simone Weil*, p. 183.

7 Ibid.

8 André Weil, *The Apprenticeship of a Mathematician* (Basel, 1992), p. 177.

9 Ibid., p. 180.

10 Ibid., p. 179.

11 Ibid., p. 184.

12 Ibid., p. 180.

13 Ibid.

14 'Baptize Me?' trans. A. Fineman, in Sylvie Weil, *Chez Les Weil: André et Simone* (Paris, 2009).

15 Robert Coles, *Simone Weil: A Modern Pilgrimage* (Reading, MA, 1987), p. 47, seems to agree with Sylvie, saying that Simone, 'usually so courageous', was not so here. It's not clear, however, why exactly it is cowardice to wish to spare a loved one from prejudice. Coles also objects, on behalf of Sylvie: 'couldn't [Simone] imagine that Sylvie might take an interest in the *spiritual* side of Jewish life . . . without being a fanatic [Simone's term]'? (emphasis added). It is a mystery, however, in what way being baptized could interfere with someone's spiritual interests in Jewish life.

16 'Baptize Me?'.

17 'Return to Sources', trans. A. Fineman, in Sylvie Weil, *Chez Les Weil*.

18 Du Plessix Gray, *Simone Weil*, p. 188.

19 J. B. Perrin and G. Thibon, *Simone Weil as We Knew Her*, trans. E. Craufurd (London, 1953), p. 24.

20 Ibid.

21 Simone Weil, *Letter to a Priest*, trans. A. Wills (London, 1953), p. 10.

22 Her assumption was commonplace at the time, and presumably never challenged by any of the priests she consulted.

23 It is worth noting that Weil, unlike some Christians, has no difficulty using the word 'God', whereas others seem unable to refer to God under any other name than 'Jesus'.

24 Weil, *Letter to a Priest*, p. 13.

25 Ibid.

26 Kant, *Religion within the Boundaries of Mere Reason*, Part 6: 'Ecclesiastical Faith Has the Pure Faith of Religion for its Supreme Interpreter', trans. A. Wood (Cambridge, 1999).

27 'Wittgenstein's Lecture on Ethics: Notes on Talks with Wittgenstein', *Philosophical Review*, LXXIV/1 (January 1965), p. 15.

28 Michael Wyschogrod, *The Body of Faith: God and the People Israel* (Northvale, NJ, 1996), p. 191.

29 In Norman Solomon, *Judaism: A Very Short Introduction* (Oxford, 1996), p. 37. Emphasis in the original.

30 Abraham Heschel, *God in Search of Man: A Philosophy of Judaism* (New York, 1983).

31 Ibid., p. 17.

32 R. Rhees, ed., *Recollections of Wittgenstein* (Oxford, 1984), p. 108.

33 Simone Weil, *Gravity and Grace,* trans. E. Craufurd (London, 1992), p. 59.

34 Compare the case of Hannah Szenes, the legendary Hungarian Zionist who abandoned the safety of Palestine, joined the British army and parachuted behind enemy lines, where she was captured, tortured and eventually shot, but never gave away any secrets to the enemy. Her mission has become an inspiration to many, and is by no means considered a quixotic failure.

35 'Indestructible', trans. A. Fineman, in Sylvie Weil, *Chez Les Weil.*

36 Simone Weil, *Waiting for God*, trans. E. Craufurd (New York, 2001), p. 73.

37 Cabaud Meaney, *Simone Weil's Apologetic Use of Literature: Her Christological Interpretation of Ancient Greek Texts* (Oxford, 2007), pp. 109–12.

38 Ibid., p. 110, n.130.

39 Simone Weil, *The Need for Roots*, trans. A. Wills (London, 1987), p. 26.

40 Ibid., p. 92.

41 Ibid., p. 150.

42 Ibid., p. 151.

43 John Hellman, *Simone Weil: An Introduction to Her Thought* (Waterloo, ON, 1982), p. 38.

44 *The Need for Roots*, p. 248.

45 Ibid., p. 221.

46 Ibid., p. 126.

47 Du Plessix Gray, *Simone Weil*, p. 207.

48 Simone Deitz has said that at the end, she on her own baptized Simone Weil. Simone apparently said, 'Go ahead, it can't do any harm' (Du Plessix Gray, *Simone Weil*, p. 207). Her accounts of exactly when this happened, however, vary. See Meaney, *Simone Weil's Apologetic Use of Literature*, p. 32, n.12, in particular: 'When asked by [Jacques] Cabaud when she had baptized Weil (whether at Middlesex Hospital in London, or upon her last visit at Ashford), Deitz said she could not remember . . . It is at the least astonishing that Deitz could forget something so important.'

49 Gabriel Marcel, 'Simone Weil', *The Month*, II/1 (July 1949), p. 18.

7 *Fêtes de la Faim*

1 Francine du Plessix Gray, *Simone Weil* (New York, 2001), p. 227.
2 Ibid., p. 212.
3 According to Robert Coles, a professor of psychiatry, it is, in any case,
   a mistaken diagnosis: 'Simone Weil was not at all like any anorectic
   patient I have met or treated, or any whom my colleagues who work
   regularly with anorectic women have described' (*Simone Weil:
   A Modern Pilgrimage*, Reading, MA, 1987, p. 27).
4 Simone Weil, *The Need for Roots*, trans. A. Wills (London, 1987),
   p. 229.
5 Leon Kass, *The Hungry Soul: Eating and the Perfecting of Our Nature*
   (New York, 1994).
6 Kass, *The Hungry Soul*, p. 125.
7 Ibid., p. 26.
8 Ibid., p. 89.
9 Ibid., p. 88.
10 Ibid., p. 13.
11 Ibid., p. 56.
12 Simone Weil, *Waiting for God*, trans. E. Craufurd (New York, 2001),
   p. 105.
13 Ibid.
14 Jacques Cabaud, *Simone Weil: A Fellowship in Love* (New York, 1964),
   p. 246.
15 Weil, *Waiting for God*, p. 105.
16 To be sure, she did write to a former student that she had once
   contemplated romance, but for most of her life, such a possibility
   was never seriously on the horizon.
17 Simone Weil, *Intimations of Christianity among the Ancient Greeks*
   (London, 1987), p. 99.
18 For a rare insight into those problems see Myles Burnyeat, 'Socratic
   Midwifery, Platonic Inspiration', *Bulletin of the Institute of Classical
   Studies*, 24 (1977).
19 'Nobody is of the opinion', writes Weil, 'that any man is innocent,
   if possessing food himself in abundance and finding someone on his
   doorstep three parts dead from hunger, he brushes past without giving
   him anything.' (*The Need for Roots*, p. 6) Yet, 'you yourself', says

Nancy Huston, 'were three-quarters starved . . . Simone, and you went your way and gave yourself nothing'. ('Letter to Simone Weil', *Longings and Belongings*, Toronto, CA, 2005, p. 87).

20 Simone Weil, *Gravity and Grace,* trans. E. Craufurd (London, 1992), p. 80.

21 *The Need for Roots*, pp. 238–9.

22 *The Notebooks of Simone Weil*, trans. A. Wills (London, 2004), p. 472.

23 Cabaud, *Simone Weil: A Fellowship*, pp. 36–7.

24 'Family Portrait', in Sylvie Weil, *Chez Les Weil: André et Simone* (Paris, 2009).

25 Cabaud, *Simone Weil: A Fellowship*, p. 123.

26 Ibid.

27 Weil, *Intimations of Christianity among the Ancient Greeks*, p. 147.

28 Ibid., p. 101.

29 Weil, *Gravity and Grace*, p. 136.

30 Ibid., p. 3.

31 Du Plessix Gray, *Simone Weil*, p. 227.

32 Ibid.

33 Kass, *The Hungry Soul*, p. 107.

34 G.E.M. Anscombe, 'On Transubstantiation', in *Ethics, Religion, and Politics, Collected Philosophical Papers*, vol. III, ed. G.E.M. Anscombe (Minneapolis, MN, 1981) p. 108.

35 Weil, *Gravity and Grace*, p. 11.

36 Weil, *Waiting for God*, p. 103.

37 Weil, *Gravity and Grace*, p. 13.

38 Simone Weil, *First and Last Notebooks,* trans. R. Rees (London, 1970), p. 286.

39 Weil, *Gravity and Grace*, p. 15.

40 According to du Plessix Gray (*Simone Weil*, p. 164), 'both Bercher and Pétrement report that Weil occasionally proposed researching a scientific method of nourishing human beings solely on sunlight and certain minerals'. If this report is accurate, it represents a different line of thought.

41 The idea is captured perfectly in the famous poem by the legendary Hungarian, Hannah Szenes, whom we met in the previous chapter, who gave up her own (young) life in her fight against the Nazis:

Blessed is the match consumed in kindling flame.
Blessed is the flame that burns in the secret fastness of the heart.
Blessed is the heart with strength to stop its beating for honor's sake.
Blessed is the match consumed in kindling flame.

42 Chris Kraus, *Aliens and Anorexia* (Cambridge, MA, 2000), p. 26.
43 Weil, *First and Last Notebooks*, p. 330. Emphasis added.
44 Ibid., p. 96.
45 Ibid.
46 Kraus, *Aliens and Anorexia*, p. 27.
47 Ibid., p. 145.
48 'A Normal Little Girl', trans. A. Fineman, in Sylvie Weil, *Chez Les Weil*.
49 Weil, *Waiting for God*, p. 27.

8 On the Jewish Question

1 See Palle Yourgrau, 'Was Simone Weil a Jew?', *Partisan Review*, LXVIII/4 (Fall 2001). See also David Stern, 'Was Wittgenstein a Jew?' in *Wittgenstein: Biography and Philosophy*, ed. J. Klagge (Cambridge, 2001).
2 In D. Raper, ed., *Gateway to God* (Glasgow, 1974), p. 153.
3 'Return to Sources', trans. A. Fineman, in Sylvie Weil, *Chez Les Weil: André et Simone* (Paris, 2009).
4 Quoted in Jeffrey Mehlman, *Emigré New York: French Intellectuals in Wartime Manhattan, 1940–1944* (Baltimore, MD, 2000), p. 89, from 'Lettres à Boris Souvarine'.
5 See Fania Pascal, 'Wittgenstein Confesses', in *Recollections of Wittgenstein*, ed. R. Rhees (Oxford, 1984).
6 Simone Pétrement, *Simone Weil: A Life*, trans. R. Rosenthal (New York, 1976), pp. 43–4.
7 Pétrement, *Simone Weil: A Life*, p. 554, n.6. Emphasis added.
8 Trans. M. Sow and P. Yourgrau (unpublished).
9 George Steiner, *No Passion Spent* (New Haven, CT, 1996), p. 172.
10 Ibid.
11 Discussion following W. Rabi, in *Simone Weil: Philosophe, Historienne, et Mystique*, ed. G. Kahn (Paris, 1978).
12 Alfred Kazin, 'A Genius of the Spiritual Life', *New York Review of Books*

(18 April 1996), p. 20.

13 Rachel Brenner, *Writing as Resistance: Four Women Confronting the Holocaust – Edith Stein, Simone Weil, Anne Frank, Etty Hillesum* (University Park, PA, 1997)

14 In Kahn, ed., *Simone Weil*.

15 Mehlman, *Emigré New York*, p. 90.

16 Ibid., p. 95.

17 Eliot, Introduction, in Simone Weil, *The Need for Roots*, trans. A. Wills (London, 1987), p. vii.

18 J. B. Perrin and G. Thibon, *Simone Weil as We Knew Her*, trans. E. Craufurd (London, 1953), p. 119.

19 Steiner, *No Passion Spent*, p. 174.

20 Pétrement, *Simone Weil: A Life*, pp. 390–92.

21 More precisely, that he had let people believe he had one Jewish grandparent, whereas the correct number was three. See Fania Pascal, 'Wittgenstein Confesses', in *Recollections of Wittgenstein*, ed. R. Rhees (Oxford, 1984).

22 'Are We Heading for the Proletarian Revolution?' (Jacques Cabaud, *Simone Weil: A Fellowship in Love*, New York, 1964, p. 85). Indeed, it is precisely one of her complaints against Judaism that membership in this faith is a 'communal', a 'collective' affair. Is she mistaken? Rabi himself, in the midst of his critical examination of Weil, draws attention to the very communality or collectivity that so alienated her: 'In Jewish [vs Weilian] mysticism there are two essential aspects: the eminently *collective* character of salvation, and the historic aspect . . . Jewish eschatology is essentially founded on the notion of *collective* salvation' (emphasis added).

23 Sylvie Courtine-Denamy, *Three Women in Dark Times: Edith Stein, Hannah Arendt, Simone Weil*, trans. G. M. Goshgarian (Ithaca, NY, 2000).

24 Ibid., p. 49.

25 Introduction to *Gravity and Grace*, p. xxviii.

26 Steiner, who condemns Weil from on high, seems to have forgotten the words he put into Adolf Hitler's mouth in the conclusion of his novel, *The Portage to San Cristóbal of A.H.* (New York, 1981), pp. 161–3: 'It was Adolf Hitler who dreamt up the master race, who conceived of enslaving inferior peoples. Lies, lies . . . [Y]our teaching . . . The only

race on earth chosen . . . The covenant of election, the setting apart of the race, *das heilige Volk* . . . To conquer its promised land, to cut down or lay in bondage all who stand in its path . . . *Your* invention. One Israel, one *Volk*, one leader.' A. Sagiv has not forgotten Steiner's words. See 'George Steiner's Jewish Problem', *Azure*, 15 (Summer 2003). And the question remains very much alive. On 7 November 2009, an article appeared in the *New York Times*, entitled 'Who is a Jew?' It records that the British Court of Appeals has ruled that 'basing school admissions [to the publicly funded religious Jews' Free School, in London] on a classical test of Judaism – whether one's mother is Jewish – was by definition discriminatory.' According to the Court, 'the requirement that if a pupil is to qualify for admission his mother must be Jewish, whether by descent or conversion, is a test of ethnicity which contravenes the Race Relations Act'.

27 D. Edmonds and J. Eidinow, *Wittgenstein's Poker* (New York, 2001), pp. 106–12.

28 Allan Nadler, 'Romancing Spinoza', *Commentary* (December 2006).

29 Gustave Thibon, 'Discussion' following W. Rabi, '*La conception Weilienne de la creation rencontre avec la Kabbale Juive*', in *Simone Weil*, ed. Kahn.

30 Introduction to *Waiting for God*, p. xv.

31 'Stuffed Carp', in Sylvie Weil, *Chez Les Weil*. A fair point. Yet Sylvie does not mention what Simone Pétrement does, that 'almost every Sunday, [Eugenie] would follow Mme Weil into the kitchen to make sure she didn't cook anything contrary to Jewish dietary laws', nor that she 'went so far as to say that she would rather see her grand-daughter dead than married to a man that was not a Jew'. To be sure, such actions would be unlikely to have traumatized Simone; yet, at the same time, they indicate that Eugenie's presence in the Weil household was not all sweetness and light.

32 Marie Cabaud Meaney, *Simone Weil's Apologetic Use of Literature: Her Christological Interpretation of Ancient Greek Texts* (Oxford, 2007), p. 38, n.37.

33 Cited by du Plessix Gray, in *Simone Weil*, p. 149.

34 Robert Coles (*Simone Weil: A Modern Pilgrimage*, Reading, MA, 1987, p. 50) reminds us, as others have, that Weil's views here resemble the so-called Marcionite heresy, and somehow believes that this in itself

refutes Weil, confusing a label with an argument. He provides none. Are we to assume that unlike Weil, he is not in the least disturbed by the massacres?

35 *Oxford NIV Scofield Study Bible: New International Edition* (New York, 1984).

36 Elaine Scarry, *The Body in Pain: The Making and Unmaking of the World* (New York, 1985), p. 208.

37 Simone Weil, *Letter to a Priest*, trans. A. Wills (London, 1953), p. 13.

38 For Robert Coles (*Simone Weil*, 'Her Jewishness'), the answer appears to be yes. Suppose, however, that Jewish theologians came to an agreement that the Holocaust was God's punishment for His people for their supposed 'sins', and that the Catholic Church were to accept this as doctrine. Weil, it is certain, would reject it, and perhaps condemn the Church (for being, again, 'too Jewish'). Would Coles step forward to accuse her, once again, of anti-Semitism?

39 Maurice Schumann, 'Discussion' following Schumann, 'Presentation of Simone Weil', in *Simone Weil*, ed. Kahn.

40 Ibid.

41 Ibid.

42 Sylvie Weil, 'Indestructible?', *Chez Les Weil*.

43 Cabaud, 'Was Simone Weil an Anti-Semite?', in *Simone Weil*, ed. Kahn.

44 Simone Weil, *Seventy Letters*, trans. and ed. R. Rees (London, 1965), p. 108.

45 Cabaud, 'Was Simone Weil an Anti-Semite?'.

46 Weil, *Letter to a Priest*, p. 64.

47 Weil, *Waiting for God*, p. 70.

48 Weil, *Seventy Letters*, p. 170.

49 Weil, *The Need for Roots*, p. 272. Emphasis added.

50 Weil, *Waiting for God*, p. 101.

51 Ibid.

52 Freud, in *Moses and Monotheism*, trans. K. Jones (New York, 1967). Freud writes, for example, that 'Moses [coming out of Egypt] had stooped to the Jews, had made them his people; they were his "chosen people" . . . Jahwe was undoubtedly a volcano-god. There was no reason for the inhabitants of Egypt to worship him' (p. 55).

53 See, for example, I. Finkelstein and N. Silberman, *The Bible Unearthed:*

Archaeology's New Vision of Ancient Israel and the Origin of Its Sacred Texts (New York, 2001).

54 Weil, *Letter to a Priest*, p. 34.

55 Sylvie Weil, '*Tzedaka*', *Chez Les Weil*.

56 Sylvie Weil, 'Return to Sources', *Chez Les Weil*.

9 The Crucifixion Suffices

1 Simone Weil, *Letter to a Priest*, trans. A. Wills (London, 1953), p. 55.

2 Strictly speaking, since Weil was not baptized (though see below), one cannot speak of heresy, but given her sympathy and closeness to the Church, the term seems appropriate.

3 In R. Rhees, ed., *Recollections of Wittgenstein* (Oxford, 1984), p. 161.

4 E. Jane Doering and Eric O. Springsted, eds, *The Christian Platonism of Simone Weil* (Notre Dame, IN, 2004), 'Introduction', Ibid., p. 4.

5 Ibid.

6 For an argument – with strong echoes of Wittgenstein – that Judaism, as opposed to Christianity, is not appropriately read as involving such ontological commitment, see Howard Wettstein, 'Doctrine', *Faith and Philosophy* (1997), and 'Against Theology', in *Philosophers and the Bible: General and Jewish Perspectives* ed. R. Eisen and C. Manekin (Bethesda, MD, 2009).

7 Michael Wyschogrod, *The Body of Faith: God and the People Israel* (Northvale, NJ, 1996), p. 190.

8 Doering and Springsted, *The Christian Platonism of Simone Weil*, p. 4.

9 Simone Weil, *Intimations of Christianity among the Ancient Greeks* (London, 1987), p. 141. Emphasis added.

10 Simone Weil, *Waiting for God*, trans. E. Craufurd (New York, 2001), p. 121.

11 Richard Sharvy, 'Plato's Causal Logic and the Third Man Argument', *Noûs*, 20 (1986), p. 523. Emphasis added.

12 Simone Weil, *Gravity and Grace*, trans. E. Craufurd (London, 1992), p. 13.

13 For discussion, in the context of Gödel's Platonism, of the intimate relationship between ontological Platonism and images of sight and light, see Palle Yourgrau, *A World Without Time: The Forgotten Legacy of*

Gödel and Einstein (New York, 2005), pp. 173–4.

14 Weil, *Intimations of Christianity among the Ancient Greeks*, p. 134.

15 Marie Cabaud Meaney, *Simone Weil's Apologetic Use of Literature: Her Christological Interpretation of Ancient Greek Texts* (Oxford, 2007), p. 101.

16 'Love is the eye of the soul.' (*Attente de Dieu* [Paris, 1966] *Waiting for God*, trans. E. Craufurd, New York, 1951).

17 Simone Weil, *The Need for Roots*, trans. A. Wills (London, 1987), p. 242. Weil herself, however, it should be said, invites misunderstanding when she says that, 'one would make a complete mistake in believing that the metaphor of the cave relates to knowledge, and that sight signifies intelligence (*Intimations of Christianity among the Ancient Greeks*, p. 134). As another image in the *Republic*, the 'divided line', makes clear, Plato believes our insight into the Good is by a faculty that provides greater contact, as it were, with reality, than what might be called 'discursive reason', the language of science (what Weil signifies here by 'intelligence').

18 See Gregory Vlastos, '"Separation" in Plato', *Oxford Studies in Ancient Philosophy*, 5 (1987), pp. 187–96.

19 For Newton, gravity constituted a kind of 'action-at-a-distance' – the sun being over there explains its attractive power on the earth over here.

20 Recall the letters sent back and forth between Simone and André, addressed to 'Dear Phenomenon' and 'Dear Noumenon'.

21 Plato, *Theaetetus*, 176a, trans. M. J. Levett (Indianapolis, IN, 1990), quoted in Weil, *Intimations of Christianity among the Ancient Greeks*, p. 77.

22 Weil, *Intimations of Christianity among the Ancient Greeks*, p. 141.

23 Ibid.

24 Ibid., p. 140. The notion of a model or *paradigma*, which Weil so powerfully invokes, is a crucial, but often neglected, concomitant to that of Form. The philosopher Aryeh Kosman gives us an insight into this notion: 'the nature of one instance of a kind is revealed by being set aside another instance [a *paradigma*] . . . a *lateral*, as it were, rather than a *vertical* form of revelation.' '[T]he hierarchical and vertical relation of [F]orm to particular', he continues, 'cannot by itself accomplish the [intellectual] clarity that Plato thinks us capable of . . . but demands . . . a lateral elucidation by some form of *paradigma*.'

('Comments on Rosen's "Is there a model of models?: paradigms in *The Statesman*"', American Philosophical Society, Eastern Meetings, Boston, December, 1994. See also Kosman, 'The Faces of Justice: Difference and Equality in Plato's *Republic*', *Boston Area Colloquium in Ancient Philosophy*, 20, 2005.)

25 Ontology and epistemology: the two axes along which the course of every philosophy, every science, is plotted. See Yourgrau, *A World Without Time*, pp. 110–14.

26 Weil, *Intimations of Christianity Among the Ancient Greeks*, p. 92: 'The artist of the very first order works after a transcendent model which he does not represent, which is only for him the supernatural source of his inspiration.'

27 Ibid., p. 147.

28 Gerard Manley Hopkins, 'Spring and Fall: To a Young Child'.

29 Weil, *Intimations of Christianity Among the Ancient Greeks*, p. 101.

30 Iris Murdoch, *The Fire and the Sun: Why Plato Banished the Artists* (New York, 1990), p. 17.

31 Weil, *Intimations of Christianity among the Ancient Greeks*, p. 166.

32 Ibid., p. 90.

33 Weil, *Waiting for God*, p. 103.

34 Weil, *The Need for Roots*, p. 140. Emphasis added.

35 Ibid.

36 'A Jewish Perspective on Incarnation', *Modern Theology*, xii/2 (April 1996), p. 204.

37 Ibid., p. 206.

38 Ibid., p. 207. Brackets added.

39 Indeed, a case could be made that the danger of idolatry is greater in Christianity than in Judaism. Jews, after all, do not worship the Chosen People as God incarnate, whereas Christians do in fact worship Jesus, a man.

40 Weil, *Letter to a Priest*, p. 16.

41 Arthur Green, in *The Brandeis Review*, xxi/2 (2001), p. 42.

42 Wyschogrod, *The Body of Faith*, p. 199.

43 Weil, *Gravity and Grace*, p. 65.

44 See Abraham Heschel, *The Prophets: An Introduction* (New York, 1969), p. 9.

45 Ibid., p. 213.

46 First Letter to the Corinthians (1 Cor. 15:17).

47 Wittgenstein, *Culture and Value*, trans. P. Winch (Chicago, IL, 1984), p. 33. Emphasis in the original.

48 Weil, *Gravity and Grace*, p. 101.

49 Ibid., pp. 58–9.

50 Three questions must be distinguished, here. Have we accurately represented Weil's conception of the incarnation of the divine in Christianity? Is Weil's account of the incarnation faithful to the Gospels? Finally, is Christianity or any doctrine of divine incarnation compelling?

51 Recall Elaine Scarry, *The Body in Pain: The Making and Unmaking of the World* (New York, 1985): for God to acquire a body is for Him to become vulnerable, as we are, to being wounded.

52 Weil, *Gravity and Grace*, p. 22.

53 Weil, *Intimations of Christianity among the Ancient Greeks*, p. 143.

54 Ibid.

55 Ibid.

56 Weil, *The Need for Roots*, p. 265.

57 Ibid., p. 210.

58 As historical speculation, Weil's judgment can be questioned. Who knows what is in the heart of a martyr, then as now? As theology, Weil's assessment is on firmer footing. If, she is saying, in their heart of hearts, the Christian martyrs believed they were guaranteed eternal life by the Resurrected Christ, that says something about the character of their devotion and their sacrifice.

59 Ibid., p. 211.

60 Weil, *Gravity and Grace*, p. 56.

61 *Recollections of Wittgenstein*, p. 111.

62 George Steiner, 'Our Homeland, the Text', in *No Passion Spent* (New Haven, CT, 1996), p. 326.

63 'Introduction', Weil, *Gravity and Grace*, p. viii.

64 Weil, *Waiting for God*, p. 69.

65 'There is a solitude of space . . .', Emily Dickinson, *Selected Poems* (New York, 1992), p. 125.

66 Wittgenstein, *Culture and Value*, p. 3.

67 Ibid., p. 26.

68 Weil, *Waiting for God*, p. 91.

69 Ibid. Recall Weil's antipathy toward the spirit animating almsgiving in America. That it is the world centre of buying and selling – i.e. capitalism – no doubt influenced her sentiments.

70 Weil, *The Need for Roots*, p. 255.

71 Ibid., p. 50.

72 Weil, *Letter to a Priest*, p. 19.

73 Ibid., p. 32.

74 Ibid., p. 10.

75 Ibid., p. 15.

76 Ibid., p. 11.

77 Weil, *Waiting for God*, p. 128.

78 Ibid.

Select Bibliography

A selection of Simone Weil's writings in French

Oeuvres Complètes, ed. André Devaux and Florence de Lussy (Paris, 1988–2002)

La Pesanteur et la Grâce (Paris, 1948)
L'Enracinement (Paris, 1949)
La Connaissance Surnaturelle (Paris, 1950)
La Condition Ouvrière (Paris, 1951)
La Source Grecque (Paris, 1953)
Venice Sauvé: Tragédie en Trois Actes (Paris, 1955)
Oppression et Liberté (Paris, 1955)
Écrits de Londres et Dernières Lettres (Paris, 1957)
Leçons de Philosophie (Paris, 1959)
Pensées sans Ordre Concernant L'amour de Dieu (Paris, 1962)
Attente de Dieu (Paris, 1966)
Sur La Science (Paris, 1966)
Poèmes, suivis de 'Venise Sauvée' (Paris, 1968)
Lettre à un Religieux (Paris, 1974)
Intuitions Pré-Chrétiens (Paris, 1985)
Premiers Écrits Philosophiques (Paris, 1988)
Écrits Historiques et Politiques: L'engagement Syndical (1927–Juillet 1934) (Paris, 1988)
Écrits Historiques et Politiques: Vers la Guerre (1937–1940) (Paris, 1989)
Écrits Historiques et Politiques: L'expérience Ouvrière e L'Adieu à La Révolution (Juillet 1934–Juin 1937) (Paris, 1991)
Cahiers (1933–Septembre 1941) (Paris, 1994)

Cahiers (Septembre 1941–Février 1942) (Paris, 1997)
Cahiers (Février 1942–Juin 1942): La Porte du Transcendant (Paris, 2002)

For a fine brief account of the genesis and publication of Weil's major writings, see Marie Cabaud Meaney, *Simone Weil's Apologetic Use of Literature* (Oxford, 2007), pp. 7–10. For an exhaustive, older but still very useful list of essays and books written by Simone Weil, in French and English, see the Bibliography to Jacques Cabaud, *Simone Weil: A Fellowship in Love* (New York, 1964). A valuable resource for essays on Weil is *Cahiers Simone Weil* (Paris), a quarterly journal published by the Association Simone Weil.

A selection of works by Simone Weil in English translation

Letter to a Priest, trans. A. Wills (London, 1953)
Seventy Letters, trans. and ed. R. Rees (London, 1965)
On Science, Necessity and the Love of God, trans. R. Rees (London, 1968)
First and Last Notebooks, trans. R. Rees (London, 1970)
Gateway to God, ed. D. Raper (Glasgow, 1974)
The Notebooks of Simone Weil, I and II, trans. A. Wills (New York, 1986)
The Need for Roots, trans. A. Wills (London, 1987)
Intimations of Christianity among the Ancient Greeks (London, 1987)
Gravity and Grace, trans. E. Craufurd (London, 1992)
Lectures on Philosophy, trans. H. Price (Cambridge, 1993)
The Simone Weil Reader, ed. G. Panichas (Wakefield, RI, 1994)
Waiting for God, trans. E. Craufurd (New York, 2001)

Works cited

Anscombe, G.E.M., 'On Transubstantiation', in G.E.M. Anscombe, *Ethics, Religion, and Politics, Collected Philosophical Papers, vol. III* (Minneapolis, 1981)

Arendt, H., *Eichmann in Jerusalem: A Report on the Banality of Evil* (New York, 1994)

Babel, I., *The Collected Stories*, ed. and trans. W. Morrison (Cleveland, OH, 1969)

Bernanos, G., *Les Grands Cimetières sous la Lune* (Paris, 1997)

Boyers, R., and P. Boyers, eds, *The New Salamagundi Reader* (Syracuse, NY, 1996)

Brenner, R. F., *Writing as Resistance, Four Women Confronting the Holocaust: Edith Stein, Simone Weil, Anne Frank, Etty Hillesum* (University Park, PA, 1994)

Burnyeat, M., 'Socratic Midwifery, Platonic Inspiration', *Bulletin of the Institute of Classical Studies*, 24 (1977)

Cabaud, J., *Simone Weil: A Fellowship in Love* (New York, 1964)

——, 'Was Simone Weil an Anti-Semite?', in *Simone Weil: Philosophe, Historienne, et Mystique*, ed. G. Kahn (Paris, 1978)

Cohen, A., ed., *Arguments and Doctrines: A Reader of Jewish Thinking in the Aftermath of the Holocaust* (New York, 1970)

Coles, R., *Simone Weil: A Modern Pilgrimage* (Reading, MA, 1987)

Courtine-Denamy, S., *Three Women in Dark Times: Edith Stein, Hannah Arendt, Simone Weil*, trans. G. M. Goshgarian (Ithaca, NY, 2000)

Dickinson, E., *Selected Poems* (New York, 1992)

Doering, E. J., and E. Springsted, eds, *The Christian Platonism of Simone Weil* (Notre Dame, IN, 2004)

Du Plessix Gray, F., *Simone Weil* (New York, 2001)

Edmonds, D., and J. Eidinow, *Wittgenstein's Poker: The Story of a Ten-Minute Argument between Two Great Philosophers* (New York, 2001)

Feferman, A., *Politics, Logic and Love: The Life of Jean van Heijenoort* (Natick, MA, 1993)

Fiedler, L., 'Simone Weil, Prophet Out of Israel: A Saint of the Absurd', in A. Cohen, ed., *Arguments and Doctrines: A Reader of Jewish Thinking in the Aftermath of the Holocaust* (New York, 1970)

——, Introduction, in Simone Weil, *Waiting for God*, trans. E. Craufurd (New York, 2001)

Finkelstein, I., and N. Silberman, *The Bible Unearthed: Archaeology's New Vision of Ancient Israel and the Origin of Its Sacred Texts* (New York, 2001)

Freud, S., *Moses and Monotheism*, trans. K. Jones (New York, 1967)

Frege, G., 'Diary: Written by professor Dr Gottlob Frege in the time from 10 March to 9 April, 1924', trans. R. Mendelsohn, ed. G. Gabriel and W. Kienzler, *Inquiry*, 39 (1996)

Hebblethwaite, P., *The Year of the Three Popes* (London, 1978)

Heijenoort, J. van, *From Frege to Gödel: A Sourcebook in Mathematical Logic,*

1879–1931 (Cambridge, MA, 1967)

Hellman, J., *Simone Weil: An Introduction to her Thought* (Waterloo, ON, 1982)

Heschel, A., *The Prophets: An Introduction* (New York, 1969)

——, *God in Search of Man: A Philosophy of Judaism* (New York, 1983)

Hitler, A., *Hitler's Table Talk: 1941–1944*, trans. N. Cameron and R. H. Steven (New York, 2000)

Huston, N., *Longings and Belongings* (Toronto, 2005)

Kant, I., *Religion Within the Boundaries of Mere Religion*, trans. A. Wood (Cambridge, 1999)

Kahn, G., ed., *Simone Weil: Philosophe, Historienne, et Mystique* (Paris, 1978)

Kazin, A., 'A Genius of the Spiritual Life', *New York Review of Books* (18 April 1996)

Kosman, A., 'Comments on Rosen, "Is There a Model of Models in Plato's *Statesman?*"' (Commentary, American Philosophical Association, Eastern Division Meetings, Boston, December 1994)

——, 'The Faces of Justice: Difference and Equality in Plato's *Republic*', *Boston Area Colloquium in Ancient Philosophy*, 20 (2005)

Kraus, C., *Aliens and Anorexia* (Cambridge, MA, 2000)

Lakatos, I., *Mathematics, Science and Epistemology* (Cambridge, 1987)

Levinas, E., *Difficult Freedom: Essays on Judaism*, trans. S. Hand (Baltimore, MD, 1990)

Malcolm, N., *Ludwig Wittgenstein: A Memoir* (Oxford, 1984)

Marcel, G., 'Simone Weil', *The Month*, II/1 (July 1949)

Meaney, M. Cabaud, *Simone Weil's Apologetic Use of Literature: Her Christological Interpretation of Ancient Greek Texts* (Oxford, 2007)

Mehlman, J., *Emigré New York: French Intellectuals in Wartime Manhattan, 1940–1944* (Baltimore, MD, 2000)

Meyerhoff, H., 'Contre Simone Weil', in *Arguments and Doctrines: A Reader of Jewish Thinking in the Aftermath of the Holocaust*, ed. A. Cohen (New York, 1970)

Milosz, C., Nobel Prize Acceptance Speech (1980)

——, *To Begin Where I Am* (New York, 2002)

Moulakis, A., *Simone Weil and the Politics of Self Denial* (Columbia, MO, 1998)

Murdoch, I., *The Sovereignty of Good* (London, 1985)

——, *The Fire and the Sun: Why Plato Banished the Artists* (New York, 1977)

Nadler, A., 'Romancing Spinoza', *Commentary* (December 2006)

Nevin, T., *Simone Weil: Portrait of a Self-Exiled Jew* (Chapel Hill, NC, 1981)

Nietzsche, F., *The Genealogy of Morals*, trans. W. Kaufman (New York,1967)

O'Brien, C. C., 'The Anti-Politics of Simone Weil', *New York Review of Books* (12 May 1977)

Oxford NIV Scofield Study Bible: New International Version, ed. C. I. Scofield (New York, 1984)

Pascal, B., *Pensées*, trans. A. J. Krailsheimer (Harmondsworth, 1966)

Pascal, F., 'Wittgenstein Confesses', in *Recollections of Wittgenstein*, ed. R. Rees (Oxford, 1984)

Perrin, J. B., and G. Thibon, *Simone Weil as We Knew Her*, trans. E. Craufurd (London, 1953)

Pétrement, S., *Simone Weil: A Life*, trans. R. Rosenthal (New York, 1976)

Plato, *The Apology*, trans. G.M.A. Grube, in Plato, *Five Dialogues* (Indianapolis, IN, 1981)

——, *The Crito*, trans. G.M.A. Grube, in Plato, *Five Dialogues*

——, *The Phaedo*, trans. G.M.A. Grube, in Plato, *Five Dialogues*

——, *The Theaetetus*, trans. M. J. Levett (Indianapolis, IN, 1990)

——, *The Republic*, trans. G.M.A. Grube (Indianapolis, IN, 1992)

Popper, K., *The Open Society and Its Enemies, vols I and II* (London, 1963)

Potok, C., *The Chosen* (New York, 1967)

Rabi, W., '*La Conception weilienne de La Création Rencontre avec la Kabbale juive*', in *Simone Weil: Philosophe, Historienne, et Mystique*, ed. G. Kahn (Paris, 1978)

Rees, L., *The Nazis: A Warning from History* (New York, 1997)

Rhees, R., ed., *Recollections of Wittgenstein* (Oxford, 1984)

Rieff, D., 'European Time', in *The New Salamagandi Reader*, ed. R. Boyers and P. Boyers (Syracuse, NY, 1996)

Sagiv, A., 'George Steiner's Jewish Problem', *Azure*, 15 (Summer 2003)

Scarry, E., *The Body in Pain: The Making and Unmaking of the World* (New York, 1985)

Schumann, M., 'Presentation of Simone Weil', in *Simone Weil: Philosophe, Historienne, et Mystique*, ed. G. Kahn (Paris, 1978)

——, 'Discussion' following Schumann, 'Presentation of Simone Weil' (1978)

Sharvy, R., '*Euthyphro* 9d–11b: Analysis and Definition in Plato and Others', *Noûs*, 6 (1972)

——, 'Plato's Causal Logic and the Third Man Argument', *Noûs*, 20 (1986)

Sophocles, *Antigone*, trans. P. Woodruff (Indianapolis, IN, 2001)

Solomon, N., *Judaism: A Very Short Introduction* (Oxford, 1996)

Spinoza, B., *Tractatus Theological-Politicus* (Leiden, 1989)

Steiner, G., *The Portage to San Cristóbal of A. H.* (New York, 1981)

——, *No Passion Spent* (New Haven, CT, 1996)

Stern, J., 'Was Wittgenstein a Jew?' in J. Klagge, ed., *Wittgenstein: Biography and Philosophy* (Cambridge, 2001)

Thom, R., '"Modern" Mathematics: An Educational and Philosophic Error?' in *New Directions in the Philosophy of Mathematics*, ed. T. Tymoczko (Boston, MA, 1985)

Vlasto, G., 'Separation', *Oxford Studies in Ancient Philosophy*, 5 (1987)

Wagon, S., *The Banach-Tarski Paradox* (New York, 1993)

Warnock, M., *Women Philosophers* (London, 1996)

Weil, A., *The Apprenticeship of a Mathematician* (Basel, 1992)

Weil, Simone, *La Connaissance Surnaturelle* (Paris, 1950)

——, *Letter to a Priest*, trans. A. Wills (London, 1953)

——, *Venise Sauvé: Tragédie en Trois Actes* (Paris, 1955)

——, *Seventy Letters*, trans. and ed. R. Rees (London, 1965)

——, *Attente de Dieu* (Paris, 1966)

——, *On Science, Necessity and the Love of God*, trans. R. Rees (London, 1968)

——, *First and Last Notebooks*, trans. R. Rees (London, 1970)

——, *Gateway to God*, ed. D. Raper (Glasgow, 1974)

——, *The Notebooks of Simone Weil, I and II*, trans. A. Wills (New York, 1986)

——, *The Need for Roots*, trans. A. Wills (London, 1987)

——, *Intimations of Christianity among the Ancient Greeks* (London, 1987)

——, '*The Iliad*: Poem of Might', in *Intimations of Christianity among the Ancient Greeks*

——, *Gravity and Grace*, trans. E. Craufurd (London, 1992)

——, *Lectures on Philosophy*, trans. H. Price (Cambridge, 1993)

——, *The Simone Weil Reader*, ed. G. Panichas (Wakefield, RI, 1994)

——, 'On Oppression and Liberty', in *The Simone Weil Reader*

——, *Waiting for God*, trans. E. Craufurd (New York, 2001)

Weil, Sylvie, *Chez Les Weil: André et Simone* (Paris, 2009)

Wettstein, H., 'Doctrine', *Faith and Philosophy* (1997)

——, 'Against Theology', in *Philosophers and the Bible: General and Jewish Perspectives*, ed. R. Eisen and C. Manekin (Baltimore, MD, 2009)

Wittgenstein, L., *Tractatus Logico-Philosophicus*, trans. D. F. Pears and B. F. McGuinness (London, 1974)

——, *Culture and Value,* trans. P. Winch (Chicago, 1984)

——, 'Wittgenstein's Lecture on Ethics', *Philosophical Review,* LXXIV/1 (January 1965)

Wyschogrod, M., *The Body of Faith*: *God and the People Israel* (Northvale, NJ, 1996)

——, 'A Jewish Perspective on Incarnation', *Modern Theology,* XII/2 (April 1996)

Yourgrau, P., 'Was Simone Weil a Jew?', *Partisan Review,* LXVIII/4 (Fall 2001)

——, *A World Without Time: The Forgotten Legacy of Gödel and Einstein* (New York, 2005)

Acknowledgements

I would like to thank Marie Cabaud Meaney and Jacques Cabaud for commenting, in detail, on the entire text, and especially Marie for her correspondence about the book. I would also like to thank Ben Callard and Mary Sullivan for their extensive comments on the text, and Miriam Schoenfield for her comments on the last two chapters. I wish also to thank Sylvie Weil for her correspondence about Simone Weil. I thank also Andrea Fineman for the assistance she provided me in translating French texts, made possible, in part, by a Norman Fund research grant provided by Brandeis University. Finally, I wish to thank Chris Kraus for her support of this project and for referring me to Reaktion Books, and to express my appreciation to Vivian Constantinopoulos at Reaktion for her expert advice at every stage on how to improve the manuscript.

Photo Acknowledgements

The author and publishers wish to express their thanks to the following sources of illustrative material and/or permission to reproduce it:

Courtesy of the Bibliothèque Nationale de France and Sylvie Weil: p. 36; courtesy Jacques Chabaud: pp. 53, 81, 83, 103, 104; photo reproduced with permission from Simone Pétrement, *Simone Weil: A Life* (New York, 1976): p. 33; photo reproduced with permission from Jacques Cabaud, *Simone Weil: A Fellowship in Love* (New York, 1964), attributed therein to Madame la Directrice: p. 47; Getty Images: p. 6; courtesy of P. Matsas: p. 90; courtesy Thomas Torres Cordova Collection: p. 149; courtesy Sylvie Weil: pp. 20, 24, 31, 55, 58, 65, 84, 85, 92, 101.